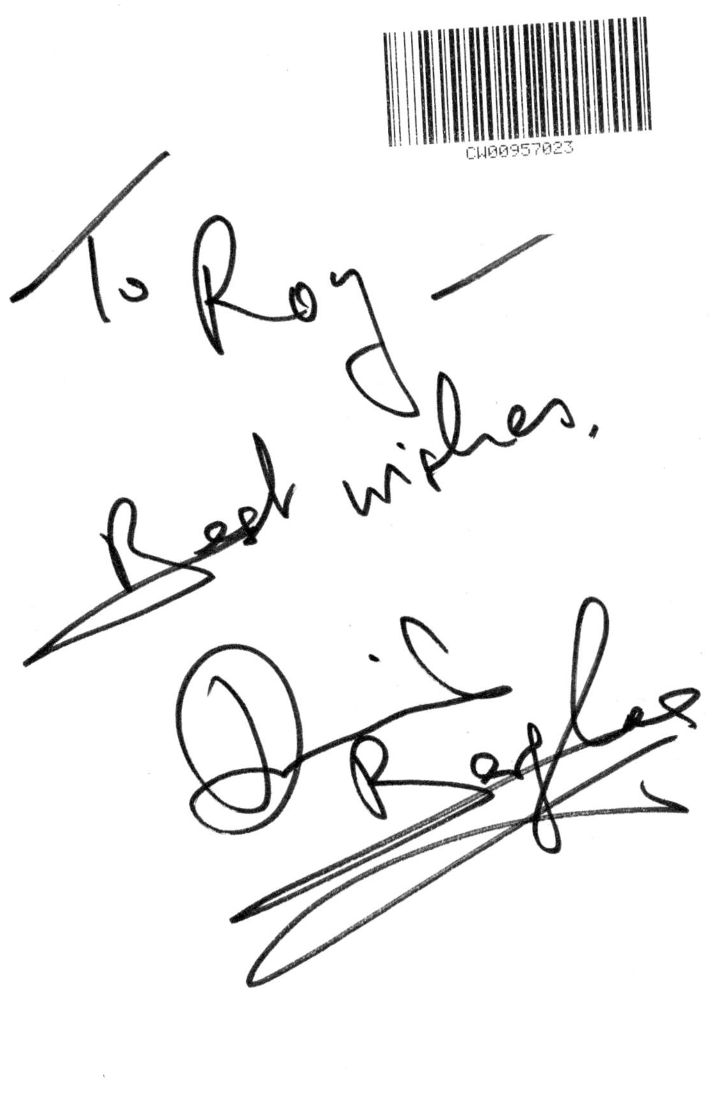
CW00957023
To Roy —
Best wishes,

A Question of Memory

by Guy Lyon Playfair

THE FLYING COW
THE INDEFINITE BOUNDARY
THE CYCLES OF HEAVEN (with Scott Hill)
THIS HOUSE IS HAUNTED
IF THIS BE MAGIC
THE HAUNTED PUB GUIDE
THE GELLER EFFECT (with Uri Geller)

A Question of Memory

David Berglas
and
Guy Lyon Playfair

JONATHAN CAPE
THIRTY-TWO BEDFORD SQUARE LONDON

First published 1988

Jonathan Cape Ltd, 32 Bedford Square, London WC1B 3EL

A CIP catalogue record for this book
is available from the British Library

ISBN 0 224 02557 0

Printed in Great Britain by
Mackays of Chatham PLC

Acknowledgments

All the original illustrations in this book were drawn by Dave James. I would also like to acknowledge my appreciation to various people I have worked with over many years: Professor Barrie Richardson, Brian Barnes, Trevor Emmett, Professor Mark Hansel, Professor Marcello Truzzi, Professor Robert Morris, Melvin Harris, Denys Parsons and, for remembering to be patient, my wife Ruth, our two sons Peter and Marvin and our daughter Irena.

David Berglas

My thanks to Dr John Beloff (University of Edinburgh), Dr Alan Gauld (University of Nottingham), Dr Erlendur Haraldsson (University of Iceland) and Dr Rupert Sheldrake for their suggestions and comments, and of course to David Berglas for fortifying my own memory system.

Guy Lyon Playfair

Contents

PART ONE

by Guy Lyon Playfair

I

The Kennedy Effect

Where were you on 22 November 1983? Without consulting diaries, most people almost certainly would not be able to remember exactly where they were on that date and what they were doing at a certain time. Yet a great many people can remember where they were on the same date twenty years previously when they heard the news that President Kennedy had been shot. Shortly after that event, it became a standard conversation-opener at parties to ask people where they were at the time and what they were doing.

My own most vivid memory is a somewhat unusual one. I was sitting on the sofa in the apartment in Rio de Janeiro that I shared with a fellow teacher named Bill Vogel. We worked different hours and at different schools, so we rarely met on weekdays. On this occasion Bill came home in the early afternoon looking unusually subdued. His exact words were:

'The President has been shot, in Texas. He was riding with Governor Connally.'

I immediately formed an image in my mind of two men in Stetson hats riding along on horseback and a shadowy figure lurking in the bushes and shooting one of them. To me, riding meant riding a horse, whereas to Bill, an American, it could also mean being driven in a motorcade, which as we were soon to know was what Kennedy had been doing when he was assassinated. All the same, that image of a pair of horse-riders ambling along a country lane has stayed in my mind, and twenty-five years later it was as clear as when it was formed. I have in fact a vivid and lasting memory of something that never happened.

This example of what we might call the Kennedy Effect

tells us something about the mysterious nature of memory. It proves how memory can play tricks with us, yet it also illustrates that it can be perfect. Once an image has been formed in the mind, it seems that it is not only easy to remember but also very difficult to forget. In extreme cases, distressing events can lead to traumas, severe emotional shocks that can cause psychological damage, and lead those suffering from them to seek psychiatric help in order to make their memories less perfect. In the right conditions, we can remember anything we choose for as long as we wish without suffering emotional distress of any kind. Fortunately, as we shall see, we can make positive use of the mechanisms that cause traumas and create perfect memories without unpleasant side-effects.

There is more to be learned from the Kennedy Effect. 'Memory', William James wrote, 'requires more than mere dating of a fact in the past. It must be dated in *my* past.' To recall a particular past epoch, he continued, 'we must think of a name or other symbol, or else of certain concrete events associated therewithal.' The association of ideas is what he considered to be the cause of both retention and recollection. The Kennedy murder is firmly implanted in my past, and it seems that I only remember it as I do because of the associations attached to it.

In his *Principles of Psychology* (1890), from which these quotations are taken, James made this observation on the workings of memory:

> The more facts a fact is associated with in the mind, the better possession of it our memory retains. Each of its associates becomes a hook to which it hangs, a means to fish it up when sunk beneath the surface. Together, they form a network of attachments by which it is woven into the entire tissue of our thought. The 'secret of good memory' is thus the secret of forming diverse and multiple associations with every fact we care to retain.

Once facts are connected by thought-relations, he concluded that 'forgetfulness is well-nigh impossible'. This is certainly true in my experience. I have only to think of Bill telling me the news of the shooting for a long chain of related memories to retrieve themselves with no effort on my part. I remember the layout of the apartment, the long climb up the steep hill that led to it, and the muffled sounds of trumpet practice coming from Bill's bedroom on Saturday afternoons. I can even remember what he often played: transcriptions of Louis Armstrong solos. That sound fishes up other memories: the many enjoyable jam sessions in which we both took part with such musicians as the veteran American expatriate Booker Pittman and a talented young local fellow named Sergio Mendes. Each of those names in turn has its own associations firmly hooked to it: standing in a Copacabana street with Booker outside the Pink Panther club where we had been playing, and listening for half the night to his fascinating life story. Thinking of Mendes and the one memorable occasion (for me, at any rate) when we played together reminds me that Bill eventually married one of the founder members of his Brazil 66 group. That memory is enough to trigger off just about the whole history of Brazilian jazz and bossa nova. So I could go on indefinitely. James's point is proved.

I could claim that I have a good memory. The only thing wrong with it is that it does not always work properly. Why, when I actually witnessed what turned out to be a burglary in progress, was I unable to give a useful description of any of the four (or was it five?) people involved? How could I have gone away for a weekend leaving my back door not only unlocked, but wide open? How did I manage to get a university degree after turning up for my first exam an hour late? It is reassuring to know that our memories can be perfect. It would be even more reassuring if they performed perfectly on demand. Often they do not.

Perhaps they might if as much attention were given in our early education to Mental Training as to Physical Training? Thinking of the hours I used to spend every week jumping up and down, swinging clubs, vaulting over wooden horses and playing all kinds of games, I cannot help wondering if some of that time would have been better spent on MT instead of PT. Memory is the basis of all learning, so it would seem logical to teach the principles of retention and recollection at the earliest possible age, especially as they are so simple. Much of my education was spent cramming my head with facts, figures and lists, but despite repeated exhortations to 'use your brain, Playfair', I was not shown how to do this systematically and efficiently.

When I was seven, I learned that there were easy ways by which to remember things. During my very first music lesson I was shown how to read music in no time at all after being told that the spaces in the bass clef were A,C,E and G which stood for All Cows Eat Grass, while the spaces in the treble clef spelled the word FACE. At about the same time my grandmother taught me that 'Thirty days hath September' and so on, the little rhyme being all that was needed for the information to stay in my mind for the rest of my life.

Such memory aids or crutches are sometimes referred to as 'mnemonic tricks'. Psychologist George A. Miller remembers being told as a schoolboy that 'memory crutches were only one grade better than cheating'. He comments:

> The idea that trickery is involved, that there is something bogus about it, has discouraged serious study of the psychological principles underlying such phenomena. Actually, some of the best 'memory crutches' we have are called laws of nature.[1]

To complain that they amount to cheating seems about as sensible as complaining that cement stops brick walls falling down. Yet the prejudice remains. In the entry for Mnemonics (memory aids) in *The Oxford Companion to the Mind* we are told that such devices are 'useless for most practical purposes'. We are also told (on the same page) that mental imagery, on which nearly all memory aid techniques are based, 'is a powerfully effective means of learning and remembering, at least under certain conditions which have not yet been fully explored'.

It is not clear to me how something not fully explored can be pronounced useless. As we shall see, the use of mental imagery not only has been very thoroughly explored, but is also clearly explained and shown to be extremely useful.

2

The Behaviour of Memory

We do not know what memory is or how it works. The dictionary description – and it is only a description and not an explanation – is 'the mental faculty of retaining and recalling past experiences'. This reminds us that there are two separate processes involved: retention and recollection. To remember something means to recall something previously retained. It follows that an important part of memory training is learning how to retain or encode properly, for there is no point in trying to recollect something that was never retained in the first place.

The faculty of retention develops long before that of recall, and is also the first to degenerate in old age. Grandparents can produce detailed and accurate memories of their childhood while forgetting what they have just been told. Under hypnosis, we can be helped to recall incidents from very early life that we could never remember in our normal conscious state, because our recall faculties were insufficiently developed when the information was received.

There is probably no such thing as a single memory system. Studies of birds and fish indicate that there may be several, each concerned with a specific sense. The octopus, for example, can have its visual memory destroyed surgically while its memory for touch remains unaffected. As for humans, a leading brain researcher, Michael S. Gazzaniga, finds that 'there are good reasons for believing that there is no unitary mechanism responsible for the encoding of information in the brain'. This may instead be 'a multifaceted process that is multiply represented in the brain'.[2]

Clearly there can be no simple explanation of the workings of memory. Bertrand Russell once described electricity as 'not a thing, like St Paul's Cathedral, but a way in which things behave'. Once we have described how it behaves, he added, we have told all we can tell about it. So it is with memory.

Memory behaves very strangely. It stores impressions in such a way that we remember some of them perfectly and forget others completely. It can be annoyingly selective. We can recall a whole poem except for a single word. (Where was that word stored, we might ask, if not with all the others?) It is also context-dependent or state-dependent, meaning that we tend to remember better when we are in the same context or state of mind as when we learned something. Police authorities often stage reconstructions of crimes or accidents in the hope that witnesses' memories will be jogged, as in the Wilkie Collins detective story *The Moonstone*.

One of Britain's leading memory researchers, Cambridge psychologist Alan Baddeley, has carried out some ingenious experiments with deep-sea divers. He made them learn lists of words on the shore and underwater, and found that when they were asked to recall them in the environment in which they were learned, their results were up to 40 per cent better than when they tried to recall on shore something learned under water or vice versa. 'It was crucial to reinstate the context if a good recall was required,' he concluded. Other researchers have shown that state-dependency is equally crucial. One group tested some heavy drinkers in the name of science and found that if they hid money or bottles while drunk they could only find them later if they were made drunk again. (On the other hand, the drunken Jack Lemmon in the film *Days of Wine and Roses* had to destroy much of a greenhouse before he could find the bottle he buried while sober.) Other experiments have shown that state-dependency applies not only to alcoholics. If we are happy or sad when we are taught something, for instance, we will remember it better when we are in the same state of mind.[3]

Memory can play tricks with us. A retrieved memory is not always the same as the one that was stored. It can even be entirely false. The psychiatrist William Sargant has described how he made use of false memories to help victims of battle shock to repair their damaged minds. They would be persuaded to relive specific experiences and recall them in vivid detail, although the experiences in question had only been suggested to them and never in fact took place.

We have, it seems, a natural ability to produce non-memories, especially under hypnosis. If asked suitable leading questions such as 'Tell me about your green teddy bear', a detailed description of one may emerge even if the subject never had one. In the 1930s it was shown how political prisoners kept in a state of stress and deprivation could be conditioned with methods derived from Pavlov's work with animals to the point where they were provided with new and artificial memories. They would then display what Sargant calls 'ultra-paradoxical behaviour' as they confessed to sins they had never committed with a great show of sincerity.[4]

In brief, what comes out of the memory system may not be what originally went in.

In the nineteenth century, things were more straightforward. According to the phrenologists, the brain was neatly mapped out with specific areas responsible for every imaginable kind of skill and emotion. It was enough to be tapped on the appropriate part of the skull for the expected results to show themselves. Memory, according to one china head I saw recently in an antique shop, was located in the middle of the forehead. This was no doubt in homage to Descartes, who considered the mind and the body to interact through the pineal gland.

Phrenology is now about as popular as the flat earth theory, and the Cartesian view of humans as dual systems runs into serious philosophical difficulties. If there were two separate worlds, mental and physical, there would presumably have to be a bridge between them, and as Professor A.J. Ayer pertinently asked in a radio talk published in 1950:

'What would the bridge consist of?'

Even so, we continue to make models of brains and minds on strictly mechanistic lines in the hope that newly discovered facts will fit them. There have been several such models in recent times. With the discovery in the 1950s of the structure of the DNA molecular chain and the claim of one of its discoverers that 'the secret of life' had been revealed, it was perhaps inevitable that a molecular model of memory would appear.

For a short time, it seemed a promising one. It even had its own journal, *The Worm Runners' Digest*, so called because many of the experiments were on flatworms. The idea was that you trained or conditioned one lot of worms, then injected some of their ribonucleic acid (RNA) into another lot which would then display the same training. The RNA molecule was known to be responsible for carrying certain kinds of information to cells such as instructions for protein synthesis, so perhaps it carried memories as well?

Apparently it did. Scientists reported that rats trained to avoid the dark could pass on this phobia to other rats via the researcher's needle. It all became rather unpleasant – one shudders at the thought of being injected with somebody else's memories – and with the death in 1977 of its leading champion, Georges Ungar, the molecular model began to fade. One of the problems it had to deal with was that nearly all the molecules in our bodies (except the DNA) replace themselves in a very short time, from a few days to a few months. Francis Crick, who shared a Nobel Prize for his DNA research, suggested that 'molecules in the synapse interact in such a way that they can be replaced by new material, one at a time, without altering the overall state of the structure'.[5] This has yet to be proved.

A more popular model is that of the brain as a hologram. With the use of laser beams and mirrors a hologram can store a huge amount of information in a small space. It has other brainlike properties: stored information can be retrieved intact even after considerable damage to part of it. We can cut pieces from both holograms and brains and still find them working almost normally. Yet, as the leading American neuropsychologist, Larry Squire, pointed out in a recent book on memory, 'Just how interference patterns, filters and coherent beams of light might be realized in the neural hardware of physiological activity of the brain has not been discussed.'[6] Even if it should remain undiscussed and unexplained, the hologram model retains some validity on the philosophical level as a description of 'the way in which things behave' in the brain.

I once attended a lecture at which a leading proponent of the brain-hologram theory, Karl Pribram, showed us a hologram recorded on a sheet of plastic. He then took a pair of scissors and cut a small piece off it. He projected the sheet again on the screen, and we saw the same three-dimensional life-like image. Pribram went on cutting bits off until the image was no longer recognisable. It was an impressive demonstration, especially in view of the fact that Pribram was a student of Karl Lashley, who did something very similar to animal brains in the course of his thirty-year search for the sites of memory traces. After numerous experiments with a variety of animals, Lashley found again and again that a learned skill was retained even after large areas of brain had been removed. He wrote: 'It is not possible to demonstrate the isolated localization of a memory trace anywhere within the nervous system.'[7]

A similar conclusion was reached by the Canadian brain surgeon Wilder Penfield after extensive exploration of the brains not of animals, but of humans. During the course of his surgical treatment of more than a thousand epileptic patients, he found that electrical stimulation of certain parts of the brain produced vivid images and detailed memories, some of which were apparently of scenes from the patient's earlier life. His initial findings were widely misinterpreted to mean that the seat of memory had at last been found. When examined more closely, however, his carefully reported research indicated otherwise.

For a start, only forty of his patients reported any imagery at all. They had all been stimulated in one or other of the temporal lobes, though a further 480 patients stimulated in the same regions produced no response, as was the case with more than six hundred who were stimulated in other areas. Moreover, it now seems likely that what was evoked in those forty patients was not genuine memory-recall. Subsequent research by others has confirmed that some kind of 'experiential response' can indeed be produced by electrical stimulation, but as Squire points out tactfully: 'The mental content elicited by stimulation is difficult to distinguish from dreams, fabricated reconstructions and fantasies.'

Penfield had originally been confident that there was a 'memory cortex' which contained the 'neuronal record', but later admitted that he was wrong. He found that apparent memories could persist even after he had cut out the entire area that had originally produced them when stimulated. 'The record is not in the cortex,' he concluded.[8]

So where is it? The conclusion of one researcher that 'memory is both everywhere and nowhere in particular' may be true, but is not helpful. Perhaps memories are not stored in the brain at all. This was the provocative view put forward by Rupert Sheldrake, a biochemist with impeccable academic qualifications, in a book published in 1981 and described by the editor of *Nature* as 'the best candidate for burning there has been for many years'. The editor's pyromaniacal tendencies were no doubt aroused by such statements as this:

> . . . not only is there no evidence that memory traces are stored in the brain, there are also reasons for thinking that no coherent mechanistic explanation of memory in terms of physical traces is possible, even in theory.[9]

Sheldrake's main objection to the mechanistic theory is, however, a perfectly reasonable one. If memories are stored in the brain, he says, then obviously there has to be a retrieval system:

> But for a retrieval system to function, it must somehow be able to recognise the appropriate memories. And to do so, it must itself have some sort of memory for what is to be retrieved. Hence the very notion of a memory retrieval system begs the question, for it presupposes what it seeks to explain.[10]

What he is suggesting is that the brain acts more like a tuning system that picks up memories than like something that stores them. Memories, he believes, are stored in a 'morphogenetic field' and retrieved by means of 'morphic resonance'. They do not reside in the brain any more than a piece of music originates in the insides of a transistor radio that is relaying it when tuned to the appropriate station. If this heretical suggestion sounds more like an act of faith than a scientific proposition, it should be remembered that mechanistic models of memory are also acts of faith. In reply to a question on the current state of the art, the head of the psychology department of the University of Edinburgh, John Beloff, had this to say:

> One can state categorically that there is as yet no accepted mechanistic theory of human memory. Presumably, every time we experience something, something is altered at the synapses in our brain cells and new connections are formed, but that is about as far as one can go.[11]

Statements such as this must not be taken to suggest that nobody knows anything at all about the brain in connection with memory. Much is known and much more is becoming known all the time. Beloff qualified his statement by adding that there has been real progress in correlating certain types of brain deficiencies or damage with certain losses of specific memory capacities. Much is also known about the various chemical and electrical events that take place when certain types of impression are received. With regard to human learning, a good deal is known about relative speeds of absorbing and retaining information, though much of this research involves the learning of nonsense syllables and so cannot be said to resemble real-life learning.

The brain may be an electro-chemical machine. What awaits explanation is how such a machine drives something as vast, diverse and creative as memory. As the Cambridge zoologist John Treherne once remarked: 'You do not understand architecture by studying the molecular structure of bricks.'

It is the architecture of memory that seems to defy rational explanation. Consider, for example, its effectiveness at bird-brain level. One of the means used by migratory birds to find their way at night is the same as that of sailors: navigation by the stars. Experiments have shown that birds raised inside a planetarium can find their way around the world when released although they have never seen the real night sky. Birds raised in fake planetariums with the stars in all the wrong places get hopelessly lost. This skill, based on memory, is all the more remarkable in that the picture of the night sky is constantly changing due to the rotation of the Earth.

Consider the ability of some kinds of salmon to find their way back to the stream where they were born after an interval of up to five years. Experiments carried out by German scientists indicate that they do this by exposure to an 'olfactory cue' or smell early in life which they can recognise up to five years later even when they have only been originally exposed to it for a few hours. How they distinguish the home-smell from all the other smells they must come across in a journey of thousands of miles is harder to explain. The fact is that they do return to their home streams at spawning time, and only then. If they come across the same olfactory cues earlier, they do not react.[12]

Certain biochemical changes in bird and fish brains have been identified that coincide with the process of 'imprinting' (early learning experience). This brings us no closer to an understanding of the architecture needed to perform feats such as those mentioned above, which seem to indicate the workings of ancestral memory. Likewise, no amount of study of the workings of human brains can account for their overall performance as both machine and creative designer. For while parts of our brains are busy running the mechanisms of our bodies, other parts are storing scraps of information, weaving them together in all possible combinations and then presenting our conscious minds with detailed plans and working drawings of which we have not the slightest knowledge until they arrive complete. We then produce a poem, a symphony or a new machine, or we act on a hunch and make a fortune. We put it down to intuition or inspiration and leave it at that.

Memories do not keep still, like jewels in a bank vault waiting to be fetched. They seem to move around, getting to know all other memories and forming associations with them. We have no conscious idea what they are up to. Whoever is doing the designing, it does not appear to be us, even though we lay personal claim to the results and behave socially as if we believe these claims when they are made by others. The concept of 'my idea' seems an irrational one on which to base the conduct of our affairs.

Solomon V. Shereshevski was a man whose memory was so remarkable that he was literally unable to forget anything. Memorising long columns of figures, complicated mathematical formulas or even poetry in a language he had never learned was no problem for him. His memory was in fact too perfect, and it led him to a state of disorientation in which he was unable to cope with the demands of everyday life. His internal designer overdid things.

A.R. Luria, the Soviet psychologist, spent more than ten years in the 1920s and 1930s studying Shereshevski's astonishing mental powers, about which he wrote a book that has become a classic in its field. Ironically, it has tended to put people off the idea of memory improvement by conveying the impression that this can lead to madness. There is no evidence whatsoever for such a fear, and there is much to be learned from the experience of a memory-prodigy described by Luria as 'a man who *saw* everything'. Here, in Shereshevski's own words, is how he saw numbers:

> Take the number 1. This is a proud, well-built man; 2 is a high-spirited woman; 3 a gloomy person (why, I don't know) . . . 7 a man with a moustache; 8 a very stout woman. As for the number 87, what I see is a fat woman and a man twirling his moustache . . .

It was the same with words. 'Each word had the effect of summoning up in his mind a graphic image,' Luria wrote, 'and what distinguished him from the more general run of people was that his images were incomparably more vivid and stable than theirs.' Any word presented to him would immediately become an image. Here is how Shereshevski tried to describe it:

> I recognise a word not only by the images it evokes but by a whole complex of feelings that image arouses. It's hard to express . . . It's not a matter of vision or hearing but some overall sense I get. Usually I experience a word's taste and weight, and I don't have to make an effort to remember it – the word recalls itself. But it's difficult to explain.[13]

It must have been. How can one explain what a word tastes like or how heavy it is? Shereshevski suffered from what is called synaesthesia or blending of the senses, which meant that he would tend to respond to a stimulus aimed at one of his senses with a reaction from one of the others, sometimes all of them. 'What a yellow, crumbly voice you have!' he once told a scientist. Different musical tones had distinctive colours for him, also shapes. 'Every sound bothers me,' he complained. 'It's transformed into a line and becomes confusing.' He once described an ordinary fence as having 'such a salty taste' and 'such a sharp, piercing sound'.

No wonder the poor fellow became confused and ended his life in what could probably have been pronounced as a form of insanity. He was hyperactive mentally, and suffered the effects of an inflated imagination, a kind of mental counterpart of the physical condition of hyperthyroidism in which an excess of hormones leads to a grotesque inflation of the body. Nevertheless, Shereshevski taught us a valuable lesson. He never trained his own memory, and had no need to do so, for it was always unusual. He seems to have discovered many of the secrets of memory training spontaneously and put them into practice with sometimes astonishing skill. For example, he once not only memorised a long string of nonsense syllables but was able to reproduce it perfectly eight years later. He also memorised the opening lines of Dante's *Divine Comedy* after hearing them only once (and not understanding a word of Italian) and recited them for Luria no less than fifteen years later. He did this by breaking each word into syllables, converting them into images of something familiar to him, and linking the images together in a long and fantastic story-line.

Sometimes he would take 'mental walks' along streets he knew well, and hang various images on the doors or windows of the buildings. Once he had placed them there, he could retrace his mental steps whenever he wished and find everything exactly where he had left it. It is interesting to note that despite the sensory confusion his synaesthesia could cause, it was always his visual sense that took charge whenever he was trying to remember something. Once he had formed a strong image, however bizarre or complicated it might be, he simply could not forget it.

It was not Shereshevski's remarkable memory that caused his mental problems, but the other way round. He had a very unusual mind early in his life, and this made it easier for him to remember things. He had other interesting abilities: long before the word 'biofeedback' was invented, he showed Luria that he was able to alter his pulse rate or the temperature of one of his hands by nothing more than concentration and visualisation. Had he been given counselling and mental training in his youth – not to improve his memory but to learn to keep it under control – he might have led a more successful life. If our memories and imaginations are completely out of control and are not guided to a specific purpose, our thinking becomes an endless stream of associations that lead nowhere. We have all probably suffered the dinner-party bore who tells us a long story in great detail, only to be reminded of yet another when it finally ends. I gave a brief demonstration of the technique with my memories fished up by the mention of Kennedy's murder, which could have continued indefinitely if I had thought they might be of interest to anybody!

We can make use of Shereshevski's methods without any fear of going off our heads. One man who did this very successfully at about the same time was a Pole named Salo Finkelstein, whose self-developed memory was studied and tested in the 1930s by American psychologist James D. Weinland.[14]

Finkelstein, a humble office clerk with what he reckoned to be a fairly average use of memory, first became interested in mental training when a stage performer came to his home town of Lodz to demonstrate his skill as a lightning calculator. He deliberately set out to imitate the entertainer by training himself, and he was so successful that before long he too was giving public demonstrations all over Europe and also in the United States.

His speciality was figures. He could memorise a thirty-digit number after looking at it for a few seconds. His method was simple: he would break the number down into groups of three or four digits, each of which had some association for him. The first three digits of the number Weinland asked him to memorise were 141, which he immediately recognised as the square root of two. The next three happened to be the last three digits of a telephone number he knew, while other groups of three or four reminded him of anything from Newton's birthdate to the number of paragraphs in Spinoza's *Ethics*.

It was obvious, Weinland noted, that Finkelstein's feats were only possible as the result of a great deal of hard work and practice. He had become so familiar with numbers that any group of digits would immediately remind him of either an association such as the year of somebody's birth or a mathematical link such as a square, cube or square root.

Unlike Shereshevski, Finkelstein apparently lived a perfectly normal life and made a successful career for himself as the result of a conscious effort to develop his mental abilities. Many others, including David Berglas, have done the same. It must be emphasised, however, that the purpose of memory training is not only to produce stage performers. It can also be used, as here, to improve our overall mental performance in everyday life both at work and in our leisure hours. The practice of jogging around the block has become popular, and those who do this every day find that they feel better for it, except when they overdo it and suffer heart attacks. A daily mental jog would bring just as much benefit with no risk of side-effects. Minds need just as much exercise as bodies, and provided they are not allowed to grow unchecked like garden weeds, as in the case of Shereshevski, the result can only be beneficial.

Alfred Russel Wallace is best remembered as the co-author with Charles Darwin of the theory of natural selection, first made public by the two of them in 1858. According to this theory, those individuals of a species who are best equipped to survive will tend to predominate over succeeding generations. Hence the phrase 'survival of the fittest'. Yet there were one or two 'residual facts', as he called them, that bothered Wallace. 'Natural selection could only have endowed savage man with a brain a little superior to that of an ape,' he wrote in 1870, 'whereas he actually possesses one very little inferior to that of a philosopher.'[15] In other words, our brains have always been much larger and more advanced in their development than they needed to be at any given stage in our evolution. Even today we seem to be using only a small portion of them.

Wallace believed that 'some more general and fundamental law underlies that of "natural selection" '. We can only speculate as to what this might be, yet it cannot be denied that our mental potential is largely unrealised and that we have presumably been provided with brains for a purpose. Even if we choose to leave religious or metaphysical aspects out of the argument, we may as well make use of our brains as best we can. Memory training is one of the quickest and easiest ways in which we can get more out of our brains, and one of the most practical. It need not be an end in itself, though. A mental system that has been made more active and efficient through exercise will repay the efforts required in a number of ways.

The most immediate benefit, naturally, will be a more useful memory. This in turn will not only help us to avoid the annoyances and occasional disasters that result from forgetfulness, but it will make the learning process a great deal easier. More important is the way in which once a mind is trained in any way it begins to perform more efficiently in every way. For example, the simple act of visualisation is the indispensable first step to any kind of mental training, and it is also now recognised as one of the essential bases of a number of self-improvement and self-healing techniques.

When we register and store an impression it does not

behave, as I have said, like the family jewels in the bank vault which will eventually be retrieved exactly as they were stored. An impression of any kind automatically becomes a potential memory, but the store in which it rests until needed is a highly dynamic zone. Memories are gregarious. They seem to want to move around and get to know other memories, as if the very act of association of any kind were instinctive. They get together with other memories to form ideas of the kind we call inspirations, which return to our conscious minds in a shape that can be quite unrecognisable. They only do this, however, if they are properly registered and stored in the first place. If not, they tend to disappear.

It seems hopeless to try to explain all this along mechanistic lines. No amount of study of electrical or chemical activities in the brain is going to tell us how memories make their own value assessments and judgments, let alone how they make their own new associations. We can only observe results, as in our dreams in which our memory stores often seem to be throwing out the day's rubbish not in a random bundle but woven into stories of their own devising, their characters sometimes transformed or associated with each other in surprising ways. A study of dreams is useful in this context because it enables us to see how memory behaves when left to its own devices. We can assume that similar processes are at work with those memories our internal architects have decided to keep for future use instead of throwing them out in the nightly dream-tale. These too are woven into sequences and groups, and can make a good deal of sense. It is hard to imagine how an electrical or chemical explanation for this selectivity and creativity could be found.

Fortunately, we have no need to explain the workings of our memory systems if we want to improve their efficiency. We merely have to observe the way in which they behave, and the two most important features of this behaviour are clearly visualisation and association. This is why the first step in memory training must be to learn to visualise and make associations. Once that step is taken, the rest is relatively straightforward.

3
A Helpful Ostrich

The vital first step is surprisingly easy, as I discovered for myself when I took my first instruction in memory-improvement from David Berglas. It was not the first time I had tried to do something about the shortcomings of my memory system, but all previous attempts had come from books and none had been entirely successful. The books all fell into one of two categories: the 'blinding with science' and the 'amaze your friends' varieties. The former were full of charts, diagrams, dramatic colour pictures and statistics from dull and artificial laboratory experiments. They tended to be more concerned with abnormal memories than with normal ones, and gave the impression that while there was still no explanation for the workings of memory, one was just around the corner.

The second variety only seemed interested in turning people into Super-memory performers who could reel off pages of telephone directories, learn all the states in the U.S.A. by heart and do all kinds of other things I had no wish to do. It was like preparing somebody for the Olympic Games before teaching them to walk, let alone run or jump. The best in this category are the books of Harry Lorayne, which are highly recommended for anybody wanting to become a professional entertainer of the Memory Man kind and also provide a solid grounding in the general principles of memory improvement. Lorayne is a skilled magician who performs such feats as reeling off the names of hundreds of people after hearing them just once as they file into the auditorium. This is impressive but not helpful to confused beginners. In my case it provoked the 'I could never do that' reaction, which is the worst possible attitude to adopt when trying to learn anything. Berglas, who regularly performs audience-memorising feats, assures me that this book is not intended to show what he can do, but what we can do.

One of the most valued books in my library is Katharine Whitehorn's *Cooking in a Bedsitter* (Penguin, 1963). Of the thousands of cookery books on the market, this is the only one I found that told me what I really needed to know at the time. When I bought it I was living in a bedsitter and I needed to know how to boil eggs, not how to produce a six-course banquet for thirty people.

David Berglas has done for my memory what Katharine Whitehorn did for my cooking. Both converted me from total ignorance to success and confidence at least at elementary levels, and both encouraged me to move on to more advanced levels. There is an important difference, however, between my cooking and my memory. It took me months of trial and error, mostly error, before I had the courage to invite somebody to sample my cooking, but I found my memory improving literally within minutes of the start of my first lesson. Before I describe exactly how this happened, I should explain how I came to be having a memory lesson from an instructor who is better known to many as a distinguished member of the entertainment profession.

David Berglas arrived in England in 1938 at the age of eleven, by which time he had attended schools in six countries and was fluent in each of their languages. His family background was so multinational that he had cousins of nine nationalities. His early interests were equally diverse, ranging from mathematics and chess to music and sport. Determined to play his part in the war effort, he joined the U.S. Army (despite never having set foot in the United States) and saw active service as an intelligence officer. His duties included attendance at the historic Nuremberg trials.

After the war he joined his family's textile firm, which had moved its base to Bradford, but a slump in the textile business forced him to find something else to do. Before long he became PT instructor at the Regent Street Polytechnic and leader of two jazz bands, while spending most of his time studying psychology at the Tavistock Clinic and attending meetings of the Magic Circle.

He became a qualified and practising psychotherapist before beginning his career as a magical entertainer, and has retained his interest in both fields to the present day. He has also found time for numerous other activities including lecturing to police groups on a number of techniques including pickpocketing, helping taxi drivers memorise the map of London, teaching water-skiing (one of his pupils became the British Olympic team coach) and creating special magical effects for a number of films, including five in the James Bond series.

In each of his two main careers David Berglas has reached huge audiences. He made his debut as a television entertainer in 1953, causing a sensation by performing sleight-of-hand illusions while wearing a short-sleeved shirt. He is generally thought to have been the first magician to have done this, and he was definitely the youngest to be awarded the Gold Star of the Inner Magic Circle.

His versatility and originality soon took him to the top of the magical profession, with regular television appearances until 1967 when he voluntarily withdrew from British screens in order to devote more time to his growing family while continuing to appear in other countries. He became known as the 'International Man of Mystery' for his wide repertoire of effects, his polished technique and such daring public stunts as hurtling down the Cresta Run and driving a car along Piccadilly – in each case securely blindfolded. A film of him performing underwater magic for the American series 'You Asked For It' was still being repeated regularly thirty years later. He was given his own half-hour programme 'Meet David Berglas' in 1955, and several subsequent series including 'The David Berglas Party', 'Magic in the Air' and in 1986 'The Mind of David Berglas'. He is a member of the governing council of the Magic Circle and a past president of the British Ring of the International Brotherhood of Magicians.

He began to practise in his second career, as a psychotherapist, on an extended visit to South Africa in 1949–50. At this time he specialised in hypnotism, although he subsequently gave it up after becoming aware of its potential dangers. His solid background in psychology has given him a wide knowledge of the human mind, which he has put to good use giving practical advice to delegates at business conferences. In fact much of his time is devoted to his executive training courses, industrial relations seminars and lectures on personal development and general efficiency for such clients as IBM, Honeywell, Coca-Cola, Ford, Glaxo, Mobil Oil and the Arts Council in addition to numerous other companies and organisations.

In 1986 I happened to hear an interview with Berglas on London's LBC radio station during the course of which he mentioned that he had long been intending to write a series of books on his various mental improvement techniques. People kept asking for such books after attending one of his courses, he said, but he had none with which to meet this steady demand. He had all the material, but had never found enough time to put it all into shape. Perhaps, he asked, there was a writer listening who might be interested in helping him?

There was, and here is the book. Before agreeing to collaborate, however, I naturally wanted to satisfy myself that Berglas had something original and useful to offer. During my first session at one of his seminars on memory improvement, it became evident that he had.

'I am going to call out a list of unconnected words,' he began. 'See how many of them you can remember. Cabbage, door, ostrich, helicopter, roller-skates . . .'

I was in trouble already. How could I possibly be expected to remember such an assortment? Why would I want to, anyway?

'. . . pencil, worm, calendar, motorway . . .'

I gave up. I had remembered the cabbage, the ostrich and the helicopter, but without even trying to remember the other words I already knew I had forgotten several of them. The list was not even finished yet.

'. . . chin, light bulb, bells.'

CABBAGE

DOOR

OSTRICH

HELICOPTER

ROLLER SKATES

PENCIL

WORM

CALENDAR

MOTORWAY

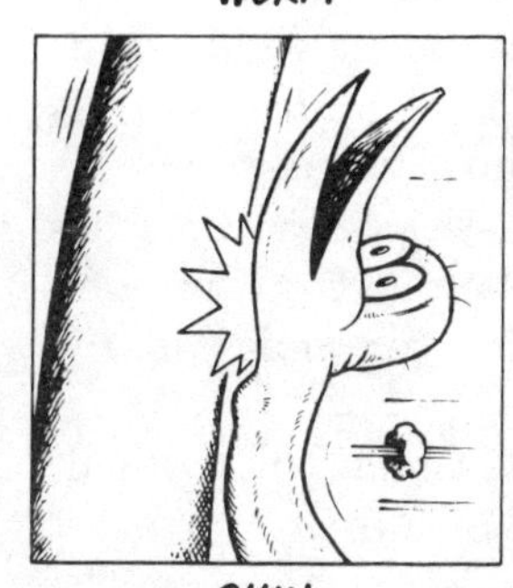
CHIN

LIGHT BULB

BELLS

My score, with much effort, was four out of twelve. Not promising, I decided. Yet Berglas gave me no chance to consider giving up after five minutes of my first lesson.

'I would not have expected you to remember all those words even if your life had depended on it,' he said, 'unless you had used a memory technique. So I will now introduce you to your first one. It is very simple yet very effective. It will enable you to remember this list, or any other, with no trouble at all.'

Berglas, whose many talents include body language-reading, must have noticed my disbelief. Again, he gave me no time for such a negative attitude to take effect but came straight to the point:

'The secret', he explained, 'is to weave a cartoon-like story that links each word to the next by using your imagination and your power of visualisation. It's always better to make up your own story, but I'll show you how I tackled this particular list when it was given to me.

'In any cartoon or story you need a central character, and I chose the ostrich as our hero. Now', the first word was CABBAGE, so imagine a cabbage patch with rows and rows of them and one enormous green CABBAGE the size of a house right in the centre. Make sure you really see it, in your mind's eye. Don't just think about it. See it.

'Now, since the cabbage is as large as a house, it is not difficult to link it to the next item on the list: DOOR. We simply visualise a large door on the cabbage.

'The door opens, and out comes the OSTRICH, who lives inside the cabbage. He is very hungry, and knows there is only one place where he can find his favourite food at this time of the year. He is in a hurry, so he jumps into his HELICOPTER and takes off. When he lands, he continues his journey in search of food on his ROLLER-SKATES and reaches his secret hiding-place, where he has left a large PENCIL. Holding this in his beak, he begins to dig holes in the ground.'

This was all rather absurd, I thought, and yet it worked. Already I had a clear picture in my mind of CABBAGE – DOOR – OSTRICH – HELICOPTER – ROLLER-SKATES – PENCIL. The words turned into images, and they stayed in my mind. That was half the list already. I was greatly encouraged.

'As you will have guessed,' Berglas went on, 'his favourite food turns out to be an especially big WORM, which pops out of one of the holes. But there is a problem: is it the worm season? The ostrich checks his CALENDAR, which is hanging nearby, and finds that unfortunately it isn't. So, still hungry, he sets off along the MOTORWAY in search of a meal. He is in such a hurry that he doesn't look where he's going, bumps his CHIN on a lamppost so hard that the LIGHT BULB falls on his head, and in true cartoon fashion he is knocked out and hears the ringing of BELLS.'

Berglas assured me that I would always be able to make up a similar nonsense story to connect absolutely any list of items. He also guaranteed that I would immediately be able to recall the whole of the list he had just given me, in its original sequence.

'Just think of the story line,' he said, 'and each word will come back to you with ease. Now, don't repeat the story but just call out the words as they come to mind.' I did so, and was astonished to find that I had made only one mistake – I left out the calendar. That was without practice, and without writing down anything at all. It took only one more run through the cartoon-story, and the list was committed to memory.

Was I a genius without knowing it?

'You may think this list was made up just to suit my story,' Berglas said, 'but I assure you it was not. In fact, the list you have just memorised was handed to me by a television producer literally moments before we went on the air. The programme was on memory, one of the popular BBC series "Body Matters", and I had been asked to demonstrate some of my techniques. During the programme, I called out the same list and then asked the large studio audience to recall as many items as they could and then to call them out. Even collectively, the audience only managed five or six. When I told them the list had to be recalled in its original sequence, there was a murmur of disbelief. Several people clearly doubted that it could be done, and I am sure they never imagined they were just about to do it – but they did.

'After I had linked the items with a story like the one I have just given you, everyone in the audience called out the complete list in unison. Then I called for a volunteer to recite the list on his or her own. A young lady raised her hand, looking very confident, and was just about to start when I asked her to recite the list backwards. To her own and everybody else's surprise, she managed it perfectly.'

If I was a genius, at least as far as memory was concerned, then clearly so was everybody else.

This was magic of a kind. Berglas had not produced a rabbit out of a hat, but he had produced something from my brain that I had not realised was there: an instinctive ability to remember things provided they are properly encoded and stored. He had also given me the magic formula, which can be expressed as $M = V+A$, or Memory = Visualisation plus Association.

I could see why there are those who feel that memory aids are a form of cheating. They make memorising too easy. Yet the critics should bear in mind that all a memory aid of the kind described here does is to reinforce the brain's natural mode of operation. It is like the push that starts the car with a flat battery, and our memory batteries have a way of going flat. As Leonardo da Vinci wrote in one of his Notebooks:

> Iron rusts with disuse, stagnant water loses its purity and in cold weather becomes frozen; even so does inaction sap the vigours of the mind.[16]

A spot of memory practice, I have found, is the ideal way to stop the mind becoming rusty, stagnant or frozen stiff. It may be even more important in this age of computers, calculators and round-the-clock television. There are those who have suggested that the human brain is undergoing a change in its functions thanks to the ubiquity of the microchip. The pessimists believe that with machines to calculate for us and television to think for us, our brains are at risk of atrophy. We can now do complicated sums by pressing buttons, involving the minimum of mental effort. Television has become a standardised force-feeding of the mind in which the viewer's participation is minimal, unlike that of the book-reader or radio-listener whose mind is constantly in action visualising the words and scenes described. Television does it all for us and reduces us to victims of hypnotic suggestion. The mind goes to sleep.

The optimists, on the other hand, foresee new opportunities for brains that have been freed from tedious routine tasks and now have the time to tackle new mental challenges, treating their computers as partners in new enterprises that they could not contemplate undertaking on their own.

Whichever proves to be right, pessimist or optimist, the need for mental exercise is an urgent one. Yet why, it may be asked, is there a need for another memory book when the basic memory-aids have been known for centuries and have not changed? The answer is that each of us interprets traditional wisdom in our own way, and Berglas presents his interpretation of age-old techniques in the most direct and accessible of ways. He concentrates on the psychological attitude required by the student of memory rather than on the various techniques.

Memory training as he practises it involves learning to think in a new way, helping the memory perform better by reinforcing natural ways of memorising rather than imposing a set of rules on it. If our memories work best with visual images and associations, then we must learn to make its task easier. We must understand what our memory systems are already doing and how they do it, then help them to do it more efficiently.

Berglas has been studying and teaching memory-improvement methods for more than forty years. He has trained his own memory to produce such impressive feats as putting the right name to each face in an audience of three hundred people, and he has passed on his secrets to the many delegates who have attended his courses. These have hitherto been restricted to executives in business, commerce and the public service. In this book, they are made available for the first time to everybody. The techniques and methods he describes are simple and enjoyable, and they work.

REFERENCES

1 George A. Miller, 'Information and Memory', *Scientific American*, 195(2), August 1956, pp.42–46.
2 M.S. Gazzaniga & J.E. LeDoux, *The Integrated Mind*, Plenum, New York, 1978.
3 A.D. Baddeley in *The Oxford Companion to the Mind* (ed. R.L. Gregory), Oxford University Press, Oxford, 1987, pp.463–4.
4 W. Sargant, *Battle for the Mind*, Heinemann, London, 1957.
5 *Nature*, 312, 1984, p.101.
6 L.R. Squire, *Memory and Brain*, Oxford University Press, Oxford, 1987, Ch.6.
7 K.S. Lashley, *Symposia of the Society for Experimental Biology*, 4, 1950, pp. 454–82.
8 W. Penfield, *The Mystery of the Mind*, Princeton University Press, Princeton, 1975, and Squire, op.cit.
9 R. Sheldrake, *A New Science of Life*, Blond & Briggs, London, 1981.
10 R. Sheldrake, 'Can our memories survive the death of our brains?', *Impressions*, 4 (4), 1986.
11 J. Beloff, Personal communication, 1987.
12 D.F. Sherry & D.L. Schacter, 'The evolution of multiple memory systems', *Psychological Review*, 94 (4), 1987, pp. 439–454.
13 A.R. Luria, *The Mind of a Mnemonist*, Jonathan Cape, London, 1969.
14 J.D. Weinland, *How to Improve Your Memory*, Harper & Row, New York, 1986.
15 A.R. Wallace, *Contributions to the Theory of Natural Selection* (2nd edn), Macmillan, London, 1871.
16 E. MacCurdy (ed.), *The Notebooks of Leonardo da Vinci*, Jonathan Cape, London, 1977.

PART TWO

by David Berglas

4
MOTIVATION AND PROGRAMMING

Memory improvement involves the development of a natural talent rather than the learning of a new skill, such as playing the piano. Even so, the most important feature of it is the same as that of any learning process, and it can be summed up in one word: motivation. Without motivation – wanting to improve the memory – the various techniques described in this book will not lead to any permanent improvement.

Much has been written about the benefits of positive thinking, and there is no doubt that it really works: I have constantly demonstrated this in my seminars. On the other hand, negative thinking also works – the more we tell ourselves that we have a bad memory the worse it will become. If we feel ill and are certain we are going to get worse, we will. This is why the great French therapist Emile Coué used to tell his patients to recite his formula 'Every day in every way I am getting better and better', which has inspired any number of successful autosuggestion and mental training programmes.

It may be difficult for somebody in a really bad way physically to persuade himself that he is getting better every day. Fortunately, however, there is no difficulty at all in persuading ourselves that our memories are getting better. As I have proved on hundreds of occasions, memory improvement is not only available to everybody of sound mind, but it can take place very quickly indeed. Considerable progress can be made in a single day, or even in a single hour. Even beginners can repeat Coué's formula with the certainty that it is true.

Having become motivated to want a better memory, the next step involves programming ourselves with the belief that we can have one. Again, this can be done quickly and easily. A good way to begin is to memorise the next telephone number you need to remember without writing it down. Instead, try visualising it and looking at its shape, converting it into something more personal than a mere string of digits. A bank card is also ideal for a first exercise of this kind, since the number is not supposed to be written down, and if you forget it, you will not get your money. Having personalised this number, by whichever of the methods to be described works best for you, you will immediately have proved to yourself that your memory really is getting better. A combination lock on a briefcase is another useful number to store in this way. Having remembered a few simple but important numbers for a few days, then for weeks and months, without any difficulty, you will gradually become aware of the infinite capacity of your memory system. Before long you will be memorising speeches, shopping lists and a day's appointments without effort. You only have to do it successfully once to know that you can do it again.

There are two ways in which motivation plays a part in memory. The first is general, as described above, and the second is specific. Let me give some examples of how this kind of motivation can occur spontaneously.

Let us suppose that you are sitting on a bus, and a couple behind are chattering away about what they did on holiday. You might be trying to read a book, and finding the conversation rather annoying as well as very dull. Then suddenly you hear them mention the name of somebody you know very well, or perhaps the name of a place you have just visited. Immediately, the conversation becomes of considerable interest, and you listen to it instead of merely hearing it. You visualise what they are saying about your friend or the place, and long after the incident you remember exactly what they said. A single word served as a trigger that suddenly motivated you automatically to pay attention, and the whole conversation is fixed in the mind, also automatically.

There is a valuable lesson to be learned from this phenomenon. If it is possible to remember so much with so little effort, through being unexpectedly triggered or motivated by a single word, it follows that we are able to choose whether a conversation (or anything else) will be remembered in detail or not. If it contains no natural trigger that motivates us to remember it, then we have to provide one. This is done by what I call 'pressing the Hot Button'.

To take an imaginary example, suppose that you are shown a photograph of nine people for just a few seconds and then asked to recall them all. The only ones easy to remember would be those who were noticeably different from the others – a woman wearing a large hat, a small bald-headed man, or somebody dressed in unusual clothes. These would remain in the mind, while the others quickly became no more than blurred images. You were not motivated to remember them clearly.

Now imagine being told that somebody had recently been to a party to which you were not invited, and had met several of your friends. 'I have a photo with me,' you are told. 'I'm not supposed to show it to you, but if you promise not to tell anyone you can have a quick look.' Your Hot Button is activated automatically. You are highly motivated to see and memorise that photo. You are curious to know who is in the picture, and wondering why you were not invited. You also know you will only see it for a short time. Keyed up in this way, you have no difficulty in remembering all the people in the picture, who was next to whom, what they were wearing, and so on.

What we have to learn in memory training is to create artificial motivations when there is no natural one. This is why we make so much use of fantasy, visualisation, association and exaggeration, all of which combine to form powerful and effective triggers that motivate our memories into action. Once we have learned to do this automatically, the most seemingly hopeless task becomes considerably easier.

One group to whom I have given memory training is that of London's taxi drivers, who have to learn what they call 'the knowledge' before they can get a licence. They have to know how to find their way to all the museums, theatres and public buildings, not to mention any one of more than twenty thousand streets. It seems impossibly difficult, yet they do it. They are, of course, highly motivated to start with at the prospect of a good secure job, and I have taught them several ways of tackling their formidable task, combining most of the techniques described in this book. I show them how to divide the city into areas, then to pick out all the squares and memorise these first before moving on to the various streets that connect them. I show them how to look for the permanent features of a square or a district, and to form vivid visual links with them whenever possible, then gradually link one area to the next until they have completed their own personal visual map of the huge city. It was only natural that a London taxi driver recently won the title of Mastermind on the popular television programme of that name. A man who has acquired 'the knowledge' can easily memorise anything he chooses, since he will have programmed himself to know that he can.

A professional mountaineer will not look in despair at a distant summit and wonder if he will ever be able to climb that far. He will divide the ascent into stages and campsites, planning them so that each is within a day's climb of the next. The well-programmed memoriser will take a similar approach to a mental problem.

Could you memorise, for instance, a whole pack of playing cards that has just been shuffled, with every card in the right order? This might seem a phenomenal feat, yet it is one I have frequently demonstrated and it becomes relatively easy when I apply this technique: I divide the 54 cards (including the two jokers) into six groups of nine, make up visual associations – which I do by translating each card into a person – and then link the six groups in a chain.

It is important to point out that when a detailed stream of memory is triggered off by some unexpected stimulus, as in the example I gave of somebody in a bus mentioning a word of interest to you, it is not the memory that has suddenly improved, but the motivation that has been strong enough to

WHERE ARE DISNEYLAND AND DISNEYWORLD? AND WHICH IS LARGER?

Walt Disney created Disney**land** (1956) near Los Angeles, California and Disney**world** (1971) near Orlando, Florida.

In order to remember which is the larger of the two and where they are located, use the following memory aids:

- **World** is obviously larger than **Land**
- Disney**land** is near Los Angeles which is known as L.A. which is conveniently the first two letters of **LAnd**
- Similarly the letters O.R.L & D appear in wORLD, ORLanDo and FlORiDa
- Disneyworld is in Orlando –

wORLD
ORLanDo
fLORiDa

activate the memory.

In memory training, as in any other activity, motivation and programming are of the greatest importance. We have seen how strong motivation can arise spontaneously and press the Hot Button. We can safely assume that strong motivation of any kind will always lead to the same result. Where motivation does not occur spontaneously, we have to get into the habit of providing it ourselves.

As for programming, this is the result of experience, beliefs, and the self-confidence that comes with the discovery that we can do something we have never tried to do before. All too often, we come across people who have become negatively self-programmed to the point where they automatically adopt an 'Oh, I could never do that' attitude. In the field of memory training, such an attitude is not only disastrous, but also quite unjustified.

We do not need to improve our memories. They are already perfect. What we need to improve is the way we use them, and we cannot do this without understanding the need for positive programming and strong motivation. Once we have fully understood this need, the rest is easy.

5
SEEING AND REMEMBERING

There is, I repeat, no such thing as a bad memory. Everything we have ever experienced through any of our senses – everything we have ever seen, heard, smelt, touched or tasted – is securely stored. Nobody needs to be taught how to store memories, it is done automatically. Yet retrieving what we need when we need it, whether the item was registered and stored a few seconds or several years earlier, is not always automatic. It can only operate at full efficiency with the use of various techniques and with practice. What I will be showing, therefore, is not only how to store memories more efficiently but also how to retrieve them instantly.

Once we learn how to operate our memories properly, we no longer forget important dates, appointments, names, faces, facts and figures or where we left our umbrellas. We find that, as our memories begin to improve, we gain confidence, learn faster, do better at examinations and interviews, develop effortless concentration and greatly increase our all-round efficiency. The whole quality of life changes for the better.

We are helped by the fact that although memory needs to be exercised, unlike a muscle it cannot be overworked or strained. The more we remember, the more we can remember, for memory is like a magic suitcase that expands every time we put something in it. There is always room for more.

The first step to a more efficient memory is to be motivated to want to improve one's use of it. Anybody reading this book must already have taken this step, since those who are perfectly satisfied with their memories would never have picked it up. The second step involves no more than some elementary learning, and most people find that learning to memorise and recall is much easier than many things they can do already. This will become evident after reading this book and doing the exercises I have suggested. The third step is practice, for it is essential to apply the techniques I will be describing. This does not mean spending hours on end with the mental equivalent of an athlete's press-ups or a musician's scales and arpeggios, for memory exercises are both simple and enjoyable. They are also of immediate practical value.

I can give every reader a guarantee with confidence. After more than thirty years of giving lectures, workshops and seminars to thousands of men, women and children, some of whom are now at the top of their professions, I have never had a single failure. Some, naturally, have benefited more than others, but there have been no dropouts. That is why I can guarantee that everybody of sound mind of any age will experience memory improvement of some degree after reading this book, or in many cases while reading it. I would, however, recommend reading the book to the end before trying any of the exercises given in the Appendix, because we can only make full use of memory aids and techniques when we have undergone a change in mental attitude and learned to approach the task of remembering in a new way. This cannot be described briefly.

I have kept technical language to the minimum. Just as anyone can learn to ride a bicycle or to swim without knowing anything at all about physics or biology, so it is possible to memorise without a specialised knowledge of psychology. The only knowledge needed is an awareness of one's own shortcomings and the determination to do something about them.

There is an old Chinese saying:

I hear and I forget
I see and I remember
I do and I understand

Much wisdom and experience went into the writing of

these lines. We still use the phrase 'in one ear and out the other', and as far as memory is concerned our sense of hearing is undoubtedly the most capricious. How often have we asked somebody to do something, and learned later that our request was not so much forgotten as never registered in the first place? The visual sense is quite different, and if I had to sum up the secret of efficient memory in a single sentence, I could not improve on the second line of the triplet: I see and I remember.

If a friend goes to see a new film or play and gives us a detailed account of it, we should have a good idea of what it is about. We might be able to give somebody else a fairly accurate description of the show we never saw but only heard about. However, if we go and see it for ourselves, our memory of it will be infinitely more durable. Many of us can clearly remember films and plays we saw thirty or forty years ago, whereas we often forget what was said to us yesterday, or even a few moments ago.

To begin with it would be helpful to learn to see properly. An easy and enjoyable way is by playing what is known as Kim's or Kelly's Game. The more players who take part the better, although it can be played on one's own.

Ask somebody to put twelve or fifteen objects on a tray and cover them with a cloth. The objects should be as unlike

each other as possible. There should not be two coins, for instance. A good collection could consist of varied items, such as a key, a watch, a paper-clip, a comb, a pencil, an egg, a torch battery, a button, an elastic band, a stamp.

The tray is then brought in, and the players take a pencil and paper and sit where they have a good view of the tray. The cloth is removed, and the players look at the objects for thirty seconds. The tray is then covered, and the players make a list of as many of the objects as they can remember. Whoever gets the most correct (and the fewest incorrect – you lose a point if you get one wrong) is the winner. If you are playing the game on your own, collect the objects and leave them covered for a while to give yourself a chance to forget them.

When people play Kim's Game for the first time, they tend to make the mistake of staring intently at each object in turn and striving to remember each one separately. It is far better just to look at the collection of objects as a whole throughout the thirty seconds, seeing it as a single image rather than as a collection of different images. I have often been invited to lecture police cadets and detectives on ways of improving their powers of observation. The first thing I tell them is that when they enter a room in which a crime may have been committed, they should begin by simply standing in the doorway and taking in the whole scene.

The secret of playing Kim's Game is the same. While your competitors are staring tensely at each object or hurriedly repeating the name of each one to themselves, try sitting calmly and letting the whole image sink into your mind. The game can be extended in many ways to make it more difficult. The viewing time can be shortened, or the number of items increased. Keep it simple to begin with, though, for this is merely practice in learning to see.

Although I recommend reading the whole of this book before trying any of the exercises, an exception can be made with this one, for it gives people a good idea how much their memory systems need improving.

WHAT IS MISSING?

6

Sight and Sound

Most instruction manuals are written on the assumption that anybody following the instructions will be able to operate the machine in question just as well as anybody else. This is a reasonable assumption in the case of a household appliance or a self-assembly kit of some kind, but it is not reasonable in the case of memory improvement, for we do not all use our memories in the same way. This is a simple fact that is generally overlooked.

Impressions are taken in by means of any one of our five senses, of which those of seeing and hearing are the most important as far as memory and learning are concerned. The fact that I have stressed the importance of seeing in the previous chapter must not be taken as implying that we cannot remember anything we hear. Of course we can, yet impressions of any kind will always be received by different people in different ways, since the degree to which each of our senses has been developed varies among individuals. People tend to show a preference for receiving information either by sight or by sound, and for recalling the information in question by means of the same sense even though all our senses naturally interact and stimulate each other. A smell of cooking can immediately bring to mind a similar smell from the distant past, and this in turn can trigger off visual memories of scenes from that particular period together with 'state-dependent' memories of our feelings at the time. If we hit ourselves on the 'funny bone' in the elbow, we can be reminded of having done the same thing many years earlier, and the sensation of pain will evoke a series of memories of the original circumstances. A sensation of taste can be equally evocative. If we discover which of our senses are relatively well-developed, or relatively undeveloped, we can then tailor our personal memory-improvement programme to our own needs.

Let us look at what happens when we store mental impressions. When we make a tape recording, the machine registers every sound that reaches it — not only the conversation we want to record but all the background noise as well. We are often surprised when playing back a recording to find how many different sounds the machine picked up of which we were not consciously aware at the time.

Likewise, our senses seem to record a great many peripheral impressions of which we may never have been consciously aware. It is as if the cells of the brain pick up and store any information that comes their way just as a tape recorder does, although the mechanisms by which they appear to do so remain largely unknown. We can assume, however, that whatever we see, hear or think produces an impression of some kind on our brains, and can do this wholly irrespective of any consciousness on our part. Such impressions can be considered indelible and permanent as long as the brain cells themselves remain intact, and there is evidence that memories can remain even after major brain surgery.

Brains can do a number of things a tape recorder cannot do. Despite their automatic recording abilities, individuals can influence the quality of the recording. Motivation, attention or interest in a subject undoubtedly strengthens the impressions that we record. The brain also seems to display a natural aptitude for association-forming – ideas or thoughts that occur to us at the same time tend to remain connected, as though the impressions they produce were recorded on the same piece of mental tape, enabling us to 'play them back' as we would play back a tape recording. We often refer to this mental playback as 'association of ideas', some of which will have been originally received by sight and others by sound.

A curious and important feature of such associations is that one can influence another. Imagine, for instance, watching a piece of film showing a dense forest, with a soundtrack of pleasant birdsong and some peaceful music. Now imagine seeing exactly the same piece of film accompanied by the kind of music favoured by makers of horror films. The same visual impression now has an entirely different meaning. The forest is no longer peaceful and soothing, but menacing and thoroughly scary. If we should happen later to hear either piece of music on its own, we would instantly recall not only the film sequence, but also our emotional reaction to it.

Some people will naturally recall more efficiently by means of one sense than another. A trained musician will have a good memory for sound just as a trained artist will have one for visual images. This is a natural consequence of learning and practice involving a good deal of repetition. Yet it is important to note that strong and lasting impressions can also be received when our conscious minds are inactive, in other words when we are not trying to remember anything at all. Indeed, studies of brain-wave patterns have shown that we are more susceptible to impressions when we are in the meditative or reverie states characterised by alpha or theta waves (approximately four to twelve cycles per second) than we are in our normal waking active state with its higher beta wave characteristics.

This can easily be proved by careful use of hypnosis, in which a subject can be fed with information that will be retained as long as required, although the person may never be consciously aware of it. Yet it is important to stress that this phenomenon takes place all the time as part of our normal everyday lives, whether we ever go near a hypnotist or not. When we take in a thought or an idea, our brains will reproduce one or the other when they have received the appropriate trigger-stimulus, which may not happen until long after the information was originally received.

I suspect that this process can go some way towards explaining the mystery of 'inspiration'. There is abundant testimony from great composers, poets and artists that some of their most successful works have 'come' to them out of the blue, often when they are in a passive and relaxed state of mind. In this state, even those of us who are not particularly creative can often be surprised by ideas that come to us. They can seem entirely new, and we may have no recollection of having previously received them.

Once lodged in the brain, an impression may lie dormant indefinitely until some discharge of mental energy takes place which recalls the original recording of the idea. This could explain many strange cases in which people have been found to possess knowledge with which they have not previously been credited. It would account for the well-known fact that people can produce ideas – whether their own or those of others – with the best intentions, unwittingly committing plagiarism in the process. It would also help answer the question of how and why important breakthroughs in scientific research are often made by two or more people independently at almost the same time, and often in wholly different parts of the world.

Although we are constantly receiving impressions, consciously or not, from our surroundings, and are registering them by means of any one of our senses, the most complete memories are those that impress themselves on all (or nearly all) of our senses at the same time. During a thunderstorm, for example, our eyes see the lightning, our ears hear the thunder and we feel the wind and the rain on our skins. Later, we smell the freshness in the air. If we are indoors and watching a thunderstorm through a soundproof window, we will obviously only be able to take in the visual features of the storm – the trees bending and the rain forming puddles, and so on. Yet we will instinctively associate what we are seeing with previous memories of what we saw, heard, smelled and touched during previous storms. We will have stored a complete piece of information that can be sensed as a whole as what we would call an atmosphere. Any one of those sights or sounds we encounter at a later date will recall all the original sensations of the storm. A single piece of information fed into our brains – perhaps just a word or a sound – can recall an entire scene, regardless of which of our senses originally recorded it.

Despite this degree of co-operation among the senses, nearly everybody has a 'dominant' sense when it comes to retention and recall, and I must now explain how we can test ourselves to find out whether we are 'sight people' or 'sound people'. I first became aware of the existence of these two groups after noticing while giving a lecture that some members of my audience would be listening with their eyes closed. When questioned later on the material I had been teaching, these same students (who had certainly not been asleep) would again close their eyes as if trying to recall some picture.

I should point out in passing that closing the eyes in concentration or staring at the ceiling is not the right way to visualise. Visualisation is something we must learn to do effortlessly whatever else we may be doing at the time – driving a car, walking along the street or talking to somebody. It involves adding a mental image to our normal waking consciousness, and not forcing ourselves into an artificial state.

Others, by contrast, would occasionally move their hands, as if conducting sounds that they were hearing inside their heads, or at least attempting to do so. This observation led me to pay more attention to the individual needs of my listeners and modify my teaching methods to include instructions for both groups.

I also noticed that people would tend to recollect a thought by the same process with which they committed it to memory. Since this appears to be a widespread and natural instinct, it seems sensible to test ourselves in order to find out which is our best remembering technique. Two people are required for this test:

THE SIGHT/SOUND TEST

1 Ask your colleague to write six to eight familiar words of one syllable on a piece of paper, making sure that there is no obvious association between any one and any other, such as cat and mat or dog and bone. Each word must represent a distinct and independent idea. A good list, for example, would be: cow, plug, hope, beat, wave and soup. There are no obvious associations between any two of those words.

2 This sheet of paper is marked A. Now ask your colleague to write the same words on another sheet of paper,

marked B, but in a different order, again making sure that they do not fall into pairs whether by sound or meaning. At this stage it is essential that you do not see either list, and also that you do not know exactly how many words have been written – six, seven or eight.

3 Now ask to see list A. Read through the list of words once only, without saying them out loud, to make sure that no sound is connected with this part of the test.

4 Give the list back and write down from memory as many of the words as you can remember, in their correct order. Do this fairly quickly, because the purpose of this part of the experiment is not to test the permanence of the impressions, but to assess the ability to understand and recall words on a relatively short-term basis. Mark your paper A-1 and give it back to your partner.

5 Your partner should now read aloud the words on list B, again just once. They should be recited with no particular emphasis, and with only brief pauses between each word.

6 Write down as many of these words as you can, again in the correct order, marking the paper B-1 and handing it back to your partner.

7 Repeat the whole experiment using a different list of words. Reverse the order to reading out loud and reading by sight, so that list C is read aloud and list D in silence.

8 Add up your four scores and see how well you did with the two lists that you saw (A and D) compared to the two you heard being read out (B and C).

If there is no great difference between them, the experiment can be done again using longer lists of (different) words. It can also be repeated, but with an interval of half an hour between seeing or hearing the words and trying to write them down. Again, it is essential to use a different word list and to alter the order between the seeing and hearing stages of the test.

A clear indication should emerge as to whether learning is more effective by sight or by sound, and this discovery can be put to practical use. Anyone who is a sound-person should not as a rule take notes when listening to something to be remembered, especially if this is something that needs to be recalled in its general sense rather than verbatim. Sound-people will learn better by listening and will need only the minimum of written notes. A sight-person, on the other hand, would be well advised to learn some kind of shorthand, or to take as many notes as possible, because the notes will serve later as triggers that will recall the original information.

Sight-persons will also tend to benefit more from reading, while sound-persons will learn better from oral instruction. Members of each group can learn from the mistakes they make in these tests. Sight-persons will find that they tend to substitute words that look similar to the original (such as 'shape' instead of 'slope') whereas sound-persons will make mistakes that sound similar to what they heard ('tack' instead of 'track').

A preference for learning by sight or by sound is no more than a preference. It does not mean that we are incapable of learning by more than one of the senses, but rather that we have a natural ability which should be encouraged and put to practical use. By remaining unaware of our preferences, we could be forcing ourselves to do something unnatural by looking instead of listening or vice versa. There is no evidence, incidentally, that either preference leads to better learning or memorising.

There may, however, be some people who are so highly sound-oriented that they will be at a slight disadvantage when it comes to improving their memories, since so much of this involves the use of visual imagination. They will need to make some extra effort, especially those who claim that they are unable to visualise. There are such people, although their claim is unjustified. We all visualise all the time. Some of us merely have to learn to do so more effectively, for memory improvement without visualisation would be almost impossible. It is all a matter of self-training or programming.

7
THE CHAIN SYSTEM

One way to remember things is to give them a meaning. How, you may ask, can we give any meaning to a long number, such as a telephone number we particularly want to remember? Or a shopping list? In a later chapter I will be explaining the use of what I have called the Figure Alphabet, which can be employed to remember any number at all, but here I will describe a few very elementary ways of finding meaning in numbers and of organising them so that they are easy to remember.

The first thing to do with a number is to look at it and see if it can be split up into groups. There may be an obvious mathematical progression, like 2468, or 24612, where $2+4=6$ and $2\times6=12$. A good many numbers can be remembered by this method, but there are also numbers that cannot be given such a simple mathematical treatment. Take the number 6342, for instance. Those who are mathematically minded might notice that this is 3×21 (63) plus 2×21 (42), but if arithmetic is not your strong point you might find it easier to divide the number into 63 and 42 and think of them as the ages of a man and his wife. Descriptions of people in newspaper stories always include their ages, which gives us a mental picture of the people concerned – 'Man, 63, Marries Woman, 42'. Now that we have a mental picture of the two numbers, it is easier to remember them. They have some meaning.

Even easier to remember would be 'Man, 93, Marries Woman, 24. That is more incongruous and therefore simpler to fix in the mind. 'Man, 93, Murders Woman, 24' would be even more dramatic. It is the incongruous and the dramatic images that are the easiest to remember.

This is only one of the many ways of splitting up numbers in order to make them meaningful, but it is a good one for the beginner to practise. Let us now think about making something else meaningful and memorable – a shopping list.

Suppose we have to buy some milk, get shoes repaired, buy a pair of gloves and a new broom, and lay in a supply of pet food. This list can be arranged in a meaningful order as follows:

1 Broom. A broom has one handle and looks like a figure 1.
2 Shoes. There are two shoes in a pair.
3 Pet food. The word pet has three letters.
4 Milk. Milk has four letters.
5 Gloves. Gloves each have five fingers.

By writing down the list in this way, visually associating each number with a particular object, we have given it a meaning and a shape it did not have before.

The list can also be arranged in simple alphabetical order: A for apples, B for bread, C for (cow's) milk, E for eggs, F for flowers, and so on. Or we can make our list into a single word: if we have to buy tea, lettuce, eggs, apples and pears we can take the first letters of each word – t,l,e,a,p – and rearrange them to make PLATE. Thus our shopping list is reduced to one five-letter word, each letter of which stands for something to be bought. It is also a word that is very easy to visualise.

It is always best to avoid trying to learn things by heart. Students cramming for an examination may feel that by learning their material word for word they are going to remember it more quickly. In a sense, they are, but the material will also leave their minds just as quickly. To remember anything for a long time, we must make sure the material enters our long-term memory, and the way to do this is to give the material some meaning. Here is a simple experiment which illustrates this particular point:

Read the following list of ten words:

1 A	6 As
2 Policeman	7 He
3 Arrested	8 Tried
4 The	9 To
5 Man	10 Escape

Repeat the list to yourself a few times, visualise the scene it describes, then cover this page and write down as many of the words as you can, making sure you get them in the right order.

Now do the same with this list:

1 Pilot	6 Siren
2 Control	7 Hose
3 Plane	8 Report
4 Tyres	9 Files
5 Fluid	10 Record

Finally, do the same with this one:

1 Bus	6 Soap
2 Mat	7 Frog
3 Light	8 Shoe
4 Force	9 Pear
5 Window	10 Nose

The scores will be revealing. Many will get the first list completely correct, because the ten words form a sentence and describe something that is easy to visualise. The second list is not quite so easy, yet the words could be strung together to make a story: a PILOT at the CONTROL of a PLANE tried to land, but the TYRES burst and FLUID escaped. He heard a SIREN from the fire engine which trained a HOSE on the plane. He had to REPORT the incident to flight control where it went into his FILES containing his RECORD. The third list is clearly much more difficult to remember. There does not appear to be any connection between the various words, which were chosen at random.

A score of eight or more for the second list, and six or more for the third, is good for a first attempt. Score the same after half an hour, without looking at the original list, and real progress is being made although there is still further to go.

Remembering the words in the third list would be a little easier if they were joined into pairs. Start by visualising a doormat on a bus, which is unusual, or a frog wearing a shoe (or a shoe shaped like a frog). In this way, more of the words will be remembered than the first time, but there will still be difficulty in linking the pairs together. Merely pairing words together will not do for more than two or three pairs. Clearly, we need a technique that enables us to link random words. This is where the system known as the Chain proves to be indispensable. It has already been described briefly in Chapter 3, but since it is one of the most useful of the basic memory-aid techniques I will describe it in more detail, using a different list of words.

Imagine that you are attending one of my seminars, and I am saying that I will call out a list of words:

Stopwatch	Bicycle	Tourist	Book	Pen
Key	Spaceship	Tape recorder	Actor	Strongman

Very few people would be able to commit the whole list to memory on first hearing, and even fewer would be able to remember the items in their original order. I could have made the task easier by saying beforehand how many words I was going to call out, thus mentally preparing the listener to expect a list of ten items. I did not, however, so most people probably panicked half way through the list and gave up any hope of remembering so many apparently unconnected items, let alone remembering them in the right order.

The secret of tackling a task like this is to be found in that Chinese phrase 'I see and I remember'. It is all too easy to forget something which was merely heard, so to make it memorable it must be made visible. This could be done by writing down the ten words and learning them by heart, but this would be difficult because the words have no particular meaning in relation to each other. Therefore, we must invent some meaning. I suggested that, when playing Kim's Game, players should look at the objects on the tray as a whole, and the same can apply to a list of items that cannot immediately be seen. In this case, instead of seeing them laid out on a tray we visualise them and link them together into a story. Then, by simply recalling the story-line, we automatically remember all the items in their original sequence. Here is an example of the kind of story we could make up to help remember this particular list:

> Imagine yourself as the timekeeper in a race, holding a large STOPWATCH in your hand. (Make it a large one, because images are much easier to remember if they are exaggerated.) As you click the stopwatch the race begins. It is a BICYCLE race in which every rider is a TOURIST. We can tell that because they are all wearing very colourful national costumes.
>
> As they ride off, we notice that each of them has a huge BOOK sticking out of his back pocket.

We have already linked the first four items, just by using the imagination and making up a rather silly story, a kind of surrealist cartoon strip in which each picture focuses on one item and leads to the next: STOPWATCH – BICYCLE – TOURIST – BOOK . . . Let us finish the story:

> Think of the BOOK as a guide-book with a route-map in it. The riders have become completely lost, so they stop, take out their PENS and start to trace the route on the map. The pens start to leak (a leaking pen is easier to visualise than a normal one) and the ink runs down the page, so they throw their pens away and feel in their pockets for something else to write with.
>
> They find a large KEY, which they dip into the spilled ink in order to finish tracing the route. The key fits a huge SPACESHIP on the road in front of them. Using the key, they go in and the first thing they see is a control panel in the middle of which there is an enormous TAPE RECORDER.
>
> Seated beside this is an ACTOR learning his lines from the tape. As soon as he has finished, he goes on stage to deliver

them, going on too long and overstaying his welcome. So the next performer on the bill, a STRONGMAN, comes up behind him, picks him up bodily and flings him into the audience.

That is a thoroughly absurd story, yet it serves a serious purpose: to help in the recollection of a list of ten items in their correct sequence, a list in which at first there seemed to be no connection between any of the items. It was made up by using the kind of imagery and association we find in dreams, cartoon strips and surrealist paintings. It is easy to remember precisely because it is exaggerated and illogical. If I had managed to make up a logical story linking all the items it would have been much harder to remember.

The list above happens to be one which I use in my seminars to teach Learning Techniques. It was made up many years ago with Trevor Emmett, who was working with me at the time. I use this and dozens of other memory-chains encoded as a series of striking images. To retrieve any one of them I only have to select the first word, in this case STOPWATCH, and the rest of the chain falls into place with no effort at all on my part.

One of the advantages of the Chain system is that once it is used to memorise a series of items, it becomes just as easy to recall the list backwards as forwards. All that need be done is to retell the story beginning with the last word:

The last word was STRONGMAN. What was he doing in the story? He was throwing the ACTOR off the stage. The actor had been learning his lines from a TAPE RECORDER inside a SPACESHIP which had been entered with the use of a KEY that had been used to write with after the PEN had begun to leak. The pen had been used to write in a BOOK belonging to a TOURIST taking part in a BICYCLE race that had been started by the click of a STOPWATCH.

There was once a popular television show in which various items could be seen moving rapidly past a window. Contestants had to remember what they were in order to win them. In such conditions, it would be difficult to invent a chain-story. There would not be time. There is, however, another way of linking objects which is known as the Stack system, because it consists of visualising all the items stacked on top of each other like an enormous totem pole. We then recall the items in their original order by starting at the bottom and moving up the stack. To recall them in reverse order we start at the top and work downwards.

This method is useful for learning short lists in a short time. It is not suitable for more than ten or twelve items. When building up a stack-image, the same use is made of dramatisation and exaggeration as in the Chain system, to ensure that the image is unusual and therefore memorable. To stack up the first few of the items listed above, we could start by seeing a very large stopwatch lying on the ground with a bicycle balanced on top of it, the rider being a tourist with a fat book on his head with a big quill pen on top of that, and so on.

That is all there is to the first of our memory-aid techniques. We shall see how useful it can be in recollecting lists of a wide variety of items. It must only be used, however, when there is no need to recall any one of the items out of sequence. It may be easy to recall a whole chain or stack, but it is not so easy to remember which, for example, was number six. It would be necessary to start at the beginning and count all the items, which would be far too time-consuming. It is essential to be able to recall anything that is needed immediately, and for remembering individual items out of sequence there is another technique which will be described in due course.

8

REMEMBERING INTANGIBLES

So far we have concentrated on ways of remembering concrete objects such as stopwatches and ostriches. However, there are many occasions when it is necessary to remember abstract concepts or intangibles. To do this, all that is required is to derive a concrete 'key-word' from the concept in question, a word that is easy to visualise and which will immediately bring the abstract concept to mind.

When I was preparing the seminar already mentioned on Learning Techniques, the first topic I wanted to talk about was Efficiency. True, we can visualise efficiency in a number of ways, but it is not easy to visualise the actual word. It is much easier to visualise a concrete object that symbolises efficiency, and the first one that seemed suitable was a stopwatch. The stereotype efficiency expert is always running around timing everything that moves with a stopwatch, so I decided that the word stopwatch in this context was going to remind me of the concept of efficiency in learning techniques.

The second concept in my presentation was to be Skill, and I chose to symbolise this with the word bicycle. We need a certain amount of skill to ride a bicycle. Likewise, each of the remaining words in the chain mentioned in the previous chapter represented something I wanted to talk about. The tourist stood for foreign languages, the book and the pen symbolised book-learning and writing techniques respectively, while the key reminded me to speak about the use of key-words. The need for spaced-out revision was visualised in the form of a spaceship, 'spaced-out' on this occasion meaning revision after having set the material aside for a few days. The tape recorder brought to mind the use of tape recordings as learning aids, while the actor's part in my story was to represent the process of learning by rote. Finally, the strongman was there to remind me of the need to make strong links between all these various associations.

There is more to be said on the subject of speeches and presentations and the important part that memory plays in both their preparation and delivery. First, the process of forming concrete key-words from abstract concepts needs looking at in more detail. It is essential to be able to take any word, however difficult it may seem, and convert it into a tangible concept which can be visualised easily. Let us take the word Law.

It is essential, when forming visual image-words, to do so in such a way that we can be sure of fixing the correct word in the memory and no other. The word 'law' seems an easy one to remember – it brings to mind images of a policeman or a judge, each of which is easy to visualise. However, we have to guarantee that we are going to remember the word 'law', not 'justice', 'legality', or any other word. To do this, we need to reinforce the image to be associated with 'law' in such a way that it will always bring the correct word to mind.

Since it is a short word, we can easily think of it as an acronym – a word formed from the first letters of other words. LAW might, for instance, stand for London's Awful Weather. We can then visualise a judge in full court regalia sitting in the middle of a London street being totally drenched by London's awful weather. It is an unlikely and incongruous image, and so it will be an easy one to remember. When the time comes to think of the correct word, the image of the judge in his soaking robes and wig will recall the fact that the word in question was abbreviated from London's Awful Weather, L – A – W. This combination of two images – the judge and London's awful weather will ensure that the correct word is retrieved.

For another example of this process of conversion of intangible into tangible image, let us take a longer word – Impossibility. The word 'impossible' can be visualised easily by thinking of an escape artist being trussed up in a sack, chained, put in a box and thrown into a river. It seems impossible for him to get out. Since the exact word we need to retrieve in due course is 'impossibili – TY', we can reinforce the image by turning the last syllable into 'tea', and as we visualise our escape artist dripping wet having extricated himself from an impossible predicament, we can picture him drinking a cup of tea. In this way, we make a firm association between 'impossible' and 'tea', so we will always retrieve the correct word, 'impossibility'.

Another way of dealing with this particular word would be to think of a busy main road full of traffic, and therefore 'impassable'. We could then see ourselves crossing this impassable road, dodging the speeding cars, and calmly sipping tea at the same time. In this case, a word will have been chosen that sounds sufficiently similar to the word to be remembered even though it is not the same.

We must feel free to distort words or parts of them in any way we like as long as it helps us form a clear image. Take the word 'unemployment', for example. The last syllable sounds much like the word 'mint', and the first four consonants are the same as those in the word 'nameplate'. We can quickly put together a picture of a queue of people standing outside the unemployment exchange, all sucking mints and standing underneath a large brass nameplate.

Let us suppose we need to remember the word 'speed'. Many people would fall into the trap of thinking this is an easy one, since they have only to imagine a racing car or a skier rushing down a slope. These images are not suitable, for they might recall any number of words – quick, car, slope or race – but not the word 'speed' itself. This word sounds similar to the word 'spied', so let us combine the two by imagining ourselves being spies who have just been spotted and are using all the speed they can muster in order to escape. This combination of speed-spied will ensure that the correct word is recalled.

Some intangible words are of course very easy to visualise without any need for reinforcement by the methods I have just described. Take 'temperature', for example, We only have to visualise ourselves with a high fever and a thermometer sticking out of our mouths, and this will instantly bring the word 'temperature' to mind. There is no need to split the word up or look for a similar one.

With a word such as 'emptiness', on the other hand, nothing could be more intangible, so we need to form an association that brings back the word. With very little alteration, we can come up with an 'empty nest', and visualise a bird flying back to its nest to find it empty.

I will have more to say on this process of playing around with words in the chapter on remembering names and faces. At this stage, it is important to become accustomed to the process of making single words memorable by whatever method seems most appropriate, always bearing in mind that the more incongruous, unlikely, and personal it is, the better.

It is also important to reinforce images as much as possible. To take some of the examples above, the word 'law' could be visualised as 'wal(l)' spelled backwards and we could add an image of an upside-down wall with a judge sitting on it. The word 'temperature' can be split into 'temper' plus 'ature' – the second half sounds like somebody sneezing ('achoo') so we can imagine ourselves in a temper because we cannot stop sneezing. The more such reinforcement, the more durable the image will become.

9
THE PEG SYSTEM

Peg methods are used to store individual items in our memories until we need to retrieve one or another of them. They are particularly useful for lists of up to twenty or thirty items which we might want to recall out of sequence; this cannot be done easily by the Chain system. There are several peg methods, and they all work on the principle of associating something new – the item to be remembered – with something already familiar.

The most popular peg method consists of rhyming words for the numbers 1 to 10, based on the nursery rhyme 'One, two, buckle my shoe'. It is a useful standard list which has proved easy to visualise and remember, and is included here because it will already be known to many people:

1 – GUN   2 – SHOE   3 – TREE   4 – DOOR   5 – HIVE
6 – STICKS   7 – HEAVEN   8 – GATE   9 – WINE   10 – HEN

Here is an easy way to fix these ten peg-images in the memory:

1 – GUN	Visualise a long rifle standing upright looking like the figure 1.
2 – SHOE	We have two feet, so we have two shoes.
3 – TREE	Imagine a big tree against the sky with three bare branches.
4 – DOOR	See a typical door with four panels and the number 4 on it.
5 – HIVE	Think of a cartoon beehive that looks like five rubber tyres stacked on top of each other.

6 – STICKS	See three sticks on the ground and another three lying across them.
7 – HEAVEN	Think of 'seventh heaven' as an angel sitting on a cloud.
8 – GATE	This is a country gate with eight bars.
9 – WINE	A bottle with just the number 9 on its label.
10 – HEN	A fat hen that has just laid ten eggs or with ten little chicks.

Having made each number into an image, we then attach the item to be remembered to the appropriate peg. I will describe ways of doing this later, after outlining some of the other peg methods, the best known of which are the Alphabet and Place Methods.

The idea of a peg alphabet is to associate each of up to twenty-six items with a word beginning with a different letter, such as A – Apple, B – Book, C – Cat, and so on. Many people will already know the radio alphabet (Able, Baker, Charlie, etc.) but this will not do as a memory aid because every word in a peg alphabet must be easy to visualise, and we cannot very well visualise an 'able'. An example of a peg list based on the letters of the alphabet is given in the Appendix, and it can be altered to make it more personal. The more personal memory aids are, the better, which may explain why the Place method has proved so durable over the centuries.

This is one of the oldest known memory aids. It was used by the Romans, and works as well today as it did two thousand years ago. It is based, as are so many memory aids, on the principle of associating an item to be remembered with something familiar, and nothing is more familiar than one's own home.

To make up a personal list of place-pegs, we visualise ourselves walking around our home. In the case of a typical house, we can start at the front door, walk into the hall, then into the living room, on to the dining room, kitchen, broom cupboard and cloakroom, then go upstairs to the landing, first and second bedrooms, bathroom and finally attic or loft. We must always think of our house in the same order.

We now associate the items we have to remember with each place. For example, let us suppose we have to buy some washing powder, some soft drinks and a lettuce, and to collect our shoes from the repair shop. We associate the washing powder with our front door, perhaps by imagining a huge pile of the stuff on the doormat after coming through the letter-box. We fill the hall with soft drinks, splashing it all over the place. We put a large lettuce in our living room on one of the armchairs. Then we move to the dining room, where we place a huge pair of shoes on the dining table.

While out shopping, we only have to think of the various places in our house and the association will come to mind. There is no need to go through the shopping list in order, because any item still to be bought will remain in our minds until we buy it and visually remove it from its associated place. As we buy the lettuce, for instance, we imagine it vanishing from the chair. When we have finished shopping, we can take a quick imaginary walk round our house and check that all the associations have been dealt with. If we forgot to collect the shoes, a glance at the dining room will remind us immediately of the association made previously with shoes.

Somebody who lives in a small apartment or even a single room can make up a place-peg list just as easily as a house-owner. Again, this must be done by moving around the room in a certain order, such as: door, table, sink, cooker, refrigerator, pedal bin, radiator, washing machine, cupboard and window. If we need a separate place-peg list for an office, we can go through a similar procedure: desk, chair, telephone, typewriter, filing cabinet, copier, waste bin, window sill, plant and light fitting. These are of course only suggestions – a place-peg list must be based on a place we know well and must always be thought of in the same order.

Another way of making up a place-peg list is to use a map of the world and associate each item to be remembered with a different country: the washing powder in France, the soft drinks in Germany, the lettuce in Spain, and so on. Many people find this a particularly useful system.

Any of the varieties of peg methods mentioned above can be made more personal in a number of ways. For instance, to somebody who lives in a house numbered 4 and goes to work every day on a number 9 bus, 4 and 9 will always bring to mind the images of 'home' and 'bus' respectively. Bingo players will be familiar with such associations as Fat Lady for 8, Legs for 11 or Two Fat Ladies 88. In these examples, the number has some visual resemblance to the peg-word.

Whatever list we decide to use, it must be learned until the correct image springs to mind as soon as we think of the number attached to it. This association must be instant if it is to be of any value – we cannot afford to say to ourselves 'Oh, let me see now, number two was shoe, wasn't it?'. A good way to learn instant associations is to write the numbers 1 to 10 on a piece of paper and then call out each word as you look at each number. Then write each number on a separate card, shuffle the cards and turn them over one by one, calling out the word as soon as you see the number. In this way, the peg-numbers are learned out of sequence.

To explain how to associate new items with a basic peg list, I invite the reader to eavesdrop on one of my actual memory seminars in which I will feature two complete beginners, Simon and Diane. I have included some of their early mistakes as examples of pitfalls to be avoided.

We decided that we were going to memorise a list of ten items suggested by the delegates themselves, by making use of the rhyming peg-words 1 – GUN up to 10 – HEN. The first word suggested was 'Brick'.

'All right,' I said. 'The first item we have to remember is a brick. How are we going to associate a brick with our peg-word for number 1, which was . . .'

'Gun,' they replied in unison. They were off to a good start, having made the 1 – GUN association automatically without pausing to think.

'Good. You are visualising a brick and also a gun. How are you going to link the two images?'

'I'm looking down the barrel of my rifle and shooting at a

brick,' was the first suggestion, from Simon.

'No,' I said. 'That won't do. Suppose you had a long list of things to remember, and I asked you later what the first one was. You would remember the peg-word GUN quite easily, and you would remember that you were shooting at something, but what? Was it a book, a box, or a brick? You're not sure.' I suggested a more direct association between gun and brick.

'How about loading your rifle with a small brick instead of a bullet? Better still, make up a little cartoon sequence: imagine yourself firing your gun into the blue and seeing a whole shower of bricks cascading up and down, building themselves into a house as they reach the ground. This combines gun and brick much more directly than an image of a gun firing at a brick.'

We moved on to item number two, and Diane suggested a Streetcar.

'A streetcar,' I repeated. (I know repetition makes tedious reading, but it is essential, especially in the early stages of memory practice.) 'We have to associate a streetcar with peg number two, which was . . .'

'Shoe.' Simon and Diane had memorised the ten rhyming peg-words without difficulty and in a very short time, as almost everybody does. Simon had also learned from his first mistake. He suggested a large shoe careering along the street, a good direct association.

'Let's dramatise the scene a little,' I said. 'We have a large shoe on the rails instead of a streetcar. There's a pole sticking out of the top to touch the cable. Let's animate the scene by filling the shoe with passengers, and having a conductor selling shoe-shaped tickets.'

For item number three (TREE), Diane suggested a Sandwich, and said she could see a monkey up a tree eating one. I said that would not do, because she might forget later what the monkey was eating, or what it was doing in the tree. 'Why bring in a monkey, anyway? It's the sandwich you have to remember.'

'How about somebody eating a tree-sandwich?' was Simon's idea. That was better. It was simpler and more unlikely, and so easier to fix in the mind. Again, I suggested animating the image, by seeing ourselves on a desert island chopping up a palm tree into slices and making sandwiches with them. To reinforce the image, there is just enough for *three* sandwiches.

The fourth word on our list was Wardrobe. Here we had a problem. We had to associate wardrobe with DOOR (four), and since a wardrobe already has a door an image of an ordinary wardrobe would not be sufficiently memorable.

'Let's be ingenious', I said, 'and build a wardrobe into the door of our small room. When somebody asks where we keep our clothes, we explain that our door is our wardrobe, with its four panels that open like four little doors. That's a simple and unusual image, and it combines four, door and wardrobe. Turning things upside down or back to front is often a good way to make a striking and memorable image.'

Item number five (HIVE) was a Flower. Again, we had the problem that hives and flowers were already associated since bees fly from one to the other. How could we introduce an unusual feature? Diane suggested a huge flower stuck in a beehive and a bee wearing it as a hat, but again I had to explain that her image was not strong enough. It was also too complicated.

'You might remember the hive and the bee, and the fact that the bee was wearing some kind of hat, but what kind of hat? It's the flower we have to remember. We need a more direct link.'

'How about a beehive made of flowers?' she said. That was much better.

We were now half way through our list, and somebody asked if we could check to see if everybody had remembered all the items so far. I rejected the idea for several reasons. One of the most important features of memory-improvement methods is that they develop confidence in the fact that we *can* remember things. If we keep backtracking and revising, we are implicitly casting doubts on our abilities, which is a negative attitude. Moreover, in real life we often have no time for revision. We have to get things right first time.

While it is true that the first dramatic or absurd picture that comes to mind is the one that works best, it must be a simple and direct one. Finding such picture-associations is only a matter of practice, and both the newcomers in the group had got the hang of it before the end of their first day's instruction. Here are the images they provided for the remaining five words in the list (all of which they suggested themselves):

Six (STICKS) – a Baby. We made a cot by piling sticks on top of each other and imagined a baby sleeping peacefully in it.

Seven (HEAVEN) – a Drinking-glass. We had a mother explaining to her child that when it rained, an old man up in heaven was pouring the contents of a drinking-glass on our heads.

Eight (GATE) – Tomato soup. We decided to paint a large wooden gate with tomato soup instead of paint, reinforcing the image by imagining the taste of the soup-paint as we drank the rest of it after finishing painting.

Nine (WINE) – an Egg. We visualised an egg going through the neck of a wine bottle. (This can actually be done as a party trick.) It made an unusual and vivid image.

Ten (HEN) – Tightrope. We imagined a hen doing a tightrope act in a circus.

Now was the time for some quick revision, and I asked everybody in the room to call out the whole list in unison, which they did: 1 – Brick, 2 – Streetcar, 3 – Sandwich, 4 – Wardrobe, 5 – Flower, 6 – Baby, 7 – Drinking-glass, 8 – Tomato soup, 9 – Egg, 10 – Tightrope.

There was only one slip-up. Somebody called out 'tightrope' for number nine. I explained that this was probably due to the fact that the image of the egg in the wine bottle had not been recorded strongly enough. After a few minutes of repetition and reinforcement, the mistake was soon corrected. I am willing to bet that everybody in the room still remembers that list today.

Earlier on the same day I had taught this group the Chain system, and I asked if anybody could remember which was the seventh item on that list. There was a pause as they began to count the links in the chain, probably saying to themselves something like 'Stopwatch, bicycle, tourist, book, pen, key, oh yes – spaceship'. It took at least ten seconds before somebody called out 'spaceship'. This was far too long. Then I asked what was item number seven on the peg-list we had just learned. The reply was instant, and unanimous: 'drinking-glass'.

The point had been made: to remember a list of items that have to be recalled in their original sequence, the Chain system is the most suitable, whereas when there is a need to recall an individual item out of sequence, we use one of the peg methods.

10

KEY WORDS

Those who have the misfortune of witnessing a serious accident or a murder sometimes suffer emotional shock, or trauma, that needs psychiatric treatment if it is not to affect the personality permanently. As such people will know, it is the shock images of the dramatic and the unexpected that are the hardest to forget. Fortunately, with memory techniques we can take advantage of the principle underlying traumatic, and therefore indelibly memorable, events: while we tend to forget the ordinary we always remember the extraordinary. We also store associations with extraordinary events automatically, such associations being as memorable as the event connected to them.

The death of President Kennedy is an example of a dramatic and unexpected event, of which the recollection triggers off a number of associated events as described at the beginning of this book. My wife Ruth and I were at the London Palladium watching Sammy Davis Jr shortly after hearing the news. Half way through his act, Davis, who had been giving a brilliant performance, came on stage in his dressing gown with tears in his eyes. 'Ladies and gentlemen,' he said, 'as you know, earlier today my very good friend Kennedy was assassinated, and I'm sure you will understand that as a personal friend I just can't go on. I hope I have your sympathy.'

I can remember exactly how the audience reacted as we all stood up and filed out quietly. I remember where we were sitting and what I was wearing. I can recall some of the muted conversations we heard as we left the building – I must have been to a theatre hundreds of times, yet I cannot easily recall any other conversations overheard as I was leaving. The fact that I can on this occasion, along with numerous other associations, proves the point that our memories can store a good deal of material involuntarily given sufficient stimulus to do so.

I have already described how one of my typical groups learned the standard rhyming peg list and used it to memorise a list of ten items. I demonstrated the principle of automatic association to the same group, asking people to invent and visualise some additional information about each item on our list, beginning with item number one – a brick. What kind of brick was it? Where was it made? We eventually decided that it was a child's toy brick, made by hand in China, measuring two by two by one inches and made from a mixture of mud and red pepper. The child was using it to build a toy garage. In no time at all we had associated seven or eight pieces of new information with our brick.

We did the same for item number two – a streetcar – and built up an image of a black streetcar with silver railings and the number 792 on its side clanking up a hill in San Francisco with thirty people on board, one of whom was playing the bagpipes. As for the sandwich – item number three – we dreamed up a vast club sandwich containing three slices of brown bread and every possible kind of luncheon meat, sprinkled with sesame seeds and being eaten by Frank Sinatra. By the time we had gone through our list of ten items, we had committed seventy or eighty new items to memory with no more effort than was required to memorise the original list. If I had told the group before hand that they were all going to memorise eighty new pieces of information in a few minutes, nobody would have believed it, yet I have proved again and again how reliable this association effect is. Once the original item is firmly committed to memory, an unlimited number of subsidiary items can be attached to it permanently. If this can be demonstrated with artificial memories of the kind I have been describing, then it proves that it certainly occurs in real life contexts.

These clusters of associations can be written down in a form which Tony Buzan has called 'Mind Maps'. The key-word is written in the middle of the paper and lines like the spokes of a wheel lead from it to individual associations. These in turn can be circled and branch out into further sub-associations – the process can go on indefinitely.

People are often surprised that I am able to give a long speech, or a seminar lasting several days, without once looking at notes. The secret is simple – it involves the use of key-words linked by the Chain system to ensure that they will be recalled in the correct order, each word being chosen to represent the topic to be included. The method involved can be used to prepare a lecture, an essay or an interview, in fact for any occasion on which it is essential that we say or write everything we intended to include. It may be helpful if I describe it in more detail.

When preparing a speech or a presentation of any kind, I begin by noting any thoughts that come to mind on pieces of paper. They may consist of a single word, a sentence, or a whole paragraph. They may have occurred to me while I was walking along the street or doing anything else. They should be written down as soon as possible. I can then sit down at my leisure and put my handful of scraps of paper on the table, going through them and picking out a key-word for each one. I then write each key-word on a small card.

These must now be arranged in some sort of order. This is easier than it may seem at first, because with any list of ideas or concepts there is usually a natural progression. Some topics will be better near the beginning, others have to be near the end. Once the cards have been laid out in sequence, it is then much easier to formulate good strong opening and closing sentences.

All that remains to be done now is to weave a story through the key-words to form a chain of images that can be easily recalled, as in the example I gave beginning with a stopwatch and ending with a strongman. Chains of up to twenty or thirty key-words can easily be made, but most presentations will be based on no more than eight or ten key words – often less.

After the all-important opening remarks (which should have been carefully rehearsed and will give the speaker confidence as well as holding the attention of the audience), it is time to recall the first key-word in the chain. This word becomes the trigger for a sub-speech or mini-speech devoted exclusively to the idea represented by the word in question. Here, the automatic association method proves very useful. Even in the unfortunate event of a mental blackout, the speaker has only to think of the next word in the chain and pick up the thread of the speech by moving into the next 'mini-speech'. Using this method makes speeches enjoyable for both speaker and audience, and it eliminates the burden of striving to remember everything that has to be included. The speaker is dealing with only one topic at a time in each sub-speech, and knows beforehand that every topic in the chain will come out in the right order. This ensures that the speech is kept fresh and informative at all times.

11

The Figure Alphabet

The Figure Alphabet is one of the most useful of the basic memory-improvement techniques. Its purpose is to help us remember any number from one to infinity. Once learned, it revolutionises our ability to remember figures, and makes it impossible for us to look at car, telephone or any other numbers in the same way again.

There are ten digits in the Arabic numeral system: 1, 2, 3, 4, 5, 6, 7, 8, 9, 0 (or 1 to 9 and 0). In the Figure Alphabet we translate these numbers into letters and as there are only ten it is not difficult. Once we have familiarised the relationship between number and letter we follow three steps:

1 Translate each digit into a letter.
2 Make a word out of these letters.
3 Create an image with this word or words.

There are of course more than ten consonants in the alphabet, but with one or two exceptions they can be fitted into ten groups. For example, the sound of the letter K and the letters QU is the same, while that of J and SH are very close. We are only concerned with consonant-sounds when using the Figure Alphabet. We use any vowels we like to make up a word, as they are 'silent' and have no values in this system.

The first five digits and their corresponding consonants are:

1 = T, 2 = N, 3 = M, 4 = R, 5 = L

There is no special reason why 1 is T or 2 is N, and so on, but to help beginners to remember which consonant-sound

1 = T	6 = J
2 = N	7 = K
3 = M	8 = F
4 = R	9 = P
5 = L	0 = Z

stands for which digit I have devised some memory aids:

1 The capital T has a single down stroke, like the figure 1.
2 A lower-case n has two down strokes.
3 A lower-case m has three down strokes.
4 The word 'fouR' ends with an R.
5 Holding out your left hand with fingers together and pointing upwards and thumb at right angles, you form an L with your thumb and first finger. Associate this L with your five fingers.

To remember a short number such as 12, all we do is translate the two digits, 1 and 2, into their respective consonant-sounds. This gives us T, N. To make a word we add the first convenient vowel that comes to mind. In this case we have a wide choice: TAN, TEN, TIN, TON or TUNE. All these words translate back to 12.

The word chosen must be one that is easy to visualise. The easiest of these is probably TIN, so the number 12 has been translated into a TIN. To give the Figure Alphabet an ever wider scope – three other 'silent' letters can be added to enable more words to be made. These are the letters H, W and Y. The word WHY is a convenient acronym to remember these letters.

NUMBER	SOUND	MEMORY AIDS		
1	T	T	THE NUMBER 1 IS PART OF THE LETTER T	T HAS ONE DOWNSTROKE
2	N	(2)	TURN 2 ON ITS SIDE TO SEE N	THE TYPEWRITTEN n HAS TWO DOWNSTROKES
3	m	(3)	TURN 3 ON IT'S SIDE TO SEE m	THE TYPEWRITTEN m HAS THREE DOWNSTROKES
4	R	FOUR	R IS THE LAST LETTER OF FOUR	THE 4 R'S: READING RITING RITHMETIC & REMEMBERING!
5	L	L	5 FINGERS FORM THE LETTER L	L = 50 IN ROMAN NUMERALS

The following letters have no numerical values

To remember the number 21, we need to make up a word using N for 2 and T for 1. Again, we have a wide choice: NAT, NET, NIT, NOT, NUT, NEAT, NIGHT, NEWT, etc. Note that in words like the last two, 'igh' and 'ew' are heard as purely vowel sounds although when written they contain the consonants g, h and w. We do not need to worry about these silent consonants. For our purposes, NIGHT is simply N linked to T by a long 'i' sound.

Again, choose whichever word comes the most readily to mind as a simple visual image.

With practice, it will soon be possible to make short words out of any combination of Figure Alphabet letters, such as

The Figure Alphabet

NUMBER	SOUND	MEMORY AIDS	
6	J	J¦L	SEE J AS THE MIRROR IMAGE OF 6
7	K	K	SEE TWO "7"s IN THE LETTER K
8	F	§	SEE A SCRIPT F AS PART OF THE NUMBER 8
9	P	9¦P	SEE P AS THE MIRROR IMAGE OF 9
0	Z	ZERO	Z IS THE FIRST LETTER OF ZERO

A E I O U (*the vowels*) H W Y (*think of WHY*)

MEMO (33), TEAM (13), LOOM (53), MEAL (35), TENT (121), LIMIT (531) or TOMATO (131). Remember that the Figure Alphabet is purely phonetic, and it is the consonants that indicate the digits. The vowel sound can be whatever comes to mind.

Here is the rest of the alphabet:

6 J looks something like the mirror image of 6.
7 A sideways-on K looks like two sevens back to back.
8 You can make a lower-case f look like part of the figure 8.
9 P looks like the mirror image of 9.
0 The first letter of Zero is Z, and the last is O.

Remember that there are alternative choices for many of the consonants. Suppose that one needs to remember the number 89, for instance. In the Figure Alphabet, this becomes FP, and we do not have many words to choose from that contain F and P. The only one that comes to mind quickly is FOP, a word not much used these days. So we can alter our P to B, which is a very similar sound, and make the words FOB, FAB or FIB. We could if we like also change F into PH, which is exactly the same sound, and come up with a word like PHOBIA, or PHOEBE.

	SOUNDS	
NUMBER	BASIC	ADDITIONAL
1	T	D
2	N	-
3	M	-
4	R	-
5	L	-
6	J	CH, SH, G (soft)
7	K	C, G (hard)
8	F	V, PH
9	P	B
0	Z	S, C (soft)

This particular number, 89, is quite a tricky one. Most other two- and three-digit numbers can be made into words without difficulty. To take a few examples at random:

67 6 and 7 is J and K. This becomes JOKE or JACK
125 T,N,L becomes TUNNEL
608 J,Z,F brings the name JOZEF or JOSEPH to mind
712 K,T,N immediately suggests KITTEN

Once familiar with the Figure Alphabet, it is possible to

memorise any number at all. If your bank card number is 3158, for example, all that needs to be done is to translate the four digits – 3,1,5,8, – into their respective letters – M, T, L and F – and then make up a word or words using only those consonant-sounds. After trying out various vowel-sounds, we come up with the word MEATLOAF, which is something easy to visualise and so ideal for this purpose. From now on this particular bank card *is* a meatloaf. Its owner can imagine cutting a slice of the meatloaf every time the card is put into the machine. That number will never be forgotten.

Translating longer numbers into Figure Alphabet key-words can require some ingenuity to start with, but it can be done with any number, however long. Let us suppose that for some reason or other it is essential to remember the exact area of Brazil, which is 3,287,203 square miles. Not many people need to know that, but some might, and it would be impressive if the figure were casually mentioned in the course of a speech or a job interview.

In this particular case, we have the consonant-sounds M,N,F,K,N,Z,M. We are never going to find a word containing all those sounds in the right order, so we have to split them up. The first four – M,N,F,K – bring the word MENFOLK to mind. (The consonant L has no value here as it is silent.) The last three – N,Z,M – can become the word NIZAM, as in the Nizam of Hyderabad. We must now combine the two words MENFOLK and NIZAM into a single image and give it some specifically Brazilian association.

This could be done by visualising a reception at the Indian Embassy in Brazil. It is a men-only event, so the room is full of menfolk eating Brazil nuts, drinking coffee, dancing the samba or doing whatever one would suppose Brazilians to be doing. In the next room, the Nizam of Hyderabad sits regally on his throne receiving visitors.

Another way of memorising this particular number would be to use the phrase MY KNIFE CAN SWIM. The hard C in 'can' has the same value as K (7) in the Figure Alphabet, and the S is the same as Z (0), while W (like H and Y) has no value at all. One can then visualise a pocket knife, swimming along with the fishes in the River Amazon.

There are times when there is no need to use the Figure Alphabet in order to remember a number. Many people will have had the experience of looking up a telephone number, dialling it and finding the line engaged or unobtainable. When they dial it again later, they have to look it up again because they made no effort to remember it the first time, but merely looked it up and dialled it mechanically. How many times do we give somebody our own number only to be asked to 'hold on a minute while I get a pencil'? Time is wasted, and our telephone bill increased, just because the other person panicked at the very thought of remembering a simple number without writing it down. A similar problem can arise at a party; we want to make a note of somebody's number when we have a glass in one hand, a sandwich in the other, and haven't got a pen.

Imagine the number to be 735–7321. I would remember this by dividing it in two and thinking of the first part as 7.35 in the morning, visualising the hands on an alarm clock in that position and hearing the alarm go off. As for 7321, seven times three is 21. A lucky example, it may be thought. This is not the case, for any other number could have been memorised with a minimum of effort. It is only necessary to do this once, and the confidence will be there to do it again.

There are times, on the other hand, when there is a need to remember lists of items considerably longer than the examples I have given of up to ten or twelve. By making use of the Figure Alphabet, the peg method can be extended indefinitely.

The majority of lists that most people normally need to remember contain ten or fewer items, and for such short lists the rhyming peg-words are ideal. It would not be practical to make up a peg-word list for numbers 11 to 20 using the rhyming method, because numbers 13 to 19 all end in 'teen'. One alternative is to invent a personal list, which I have found to work very well over the years. An easy way to do this is to look around the room and choose personal objects to represent each number, perhaps a favourite picture for 11, a plant for 12, a carpet for 13 and so on. Personal associations are always the easiest to remember, and if any number has a special significance it can be added to the list. Birthdays can be useful in this respect – for someone born on the 15th, for instance, the number 15 can be visualised as 'their birthday' and the object to be remembered can be imagined as their birthday present.

A sports fan would be unable to see the number 15 without thinking of a rubgy football team, just as the number 11 automatically brings the image of a cricket team to mind. Darts players can use a dart board as peg-image for number 20, the number at the top of the board. Anybody, whatever their interests, can find numbers of personal significance, whether they are of birthdays, house or bus numbers or whatever.

From experience, I have found my personal peg-word list to work very well up to number 30. For higher numbers, I prefer to make use of the Figure Alphabet, which offers a wide choice of peg-words for each number. To make up a word to represent number 31, for example, the digits 3 and 1 become M and T (or D). By adding some vowels or silent consonants we have a number of possible words such as MAT, MUD, MAD, MOOD, MEAT, MOAT, MAID. All of these are easily visualised, so it is a matter of personal choice as to which one is used to represent 31.

In the Appendix there is a list of suggested words for all the numbers up to 100. It could be extended up to 999 with single words, but for numbers of four or more digits it is usually necessary to use two or more words, as in the example given earlier of MENFOLK NIZAM or MY KNIFE CAN SWIM for the number 3,287,203. The numbers 1 to 20 are also included, for there is no reason not to make up key-words for these as well by using the Figure Alphabet. It is a question of personal choice. Some will find it convenient to have a variety of different peg lists at their disposal, as aids in memorising different kinds of list – perhaps a rhyming peg list for up to ten items, a personal list for up to twenty, and a list based on the Figure Alphabet for more than twenty. Suggested words for numbers 00 to 09 are also included, as these can be useful for remembering fractions such as 2.03, as well as telephone code numbers.

The great advantage of key-words based on the Figure Alphabet is that there is no need to learn them by heart. Anybody who has learned the alphabet will be able to make an automatic association between any number and the corresponding consonant-sounds.

12
NAMES AND FACES

Most people have good memories for faces. To demonstrate how surprising this natural visual memory can be, I often carry out an experiment in which I show a series of fifty or sixty photographs of people very quickly, one after the other. Then I insert four or five photographs that were not shown previously and go through the same set again. Invariably, everybody instantly picks out the faces they had not seen before. One could argue therefore that all the other faces were remembered, which is partly true – they have been taken in, but this does not mean that they can all be recalled and described in detail. All the same, an impression has been retained although the pictures were only seen for a couple of seconds.

Many of us have had the experience of meeting somebody whom we have not seen for years and immediately recognising the face. Retrieving the correct name to go with it, however, is another matter. There are even those who have great difficulty in remembering the names of people they see frequently, which can be embarrassing to both parties. Remembering the name correctly is a form of flattery, whereas forgetting one implies that the person in question was not worth remembering. If this happens to us personally, we cannot help feeling slightly offended.

It is common practice in the United States for senior executives to learn the names of all their employees and to greet them by name when they meet them. It is a small gesture but a very effective one. It helps create good feelings, especially among junior employees who are flattered that the boss remembers who they are.

The secret of remembering names and faces can be summed up in the three words IMPRESSION, REPETITION and ASSOCIATION. I sometimes refer to it as the I–R–A method. (Think of the well-known abbreviation IRA.)

IMPRESSION. When meeting somebody for the first time, take a really good look at them. Look for the permanent features such as general bone structure and the size and shape of heads, eyes, noses, ears and mouths, each of these can vary considerably.

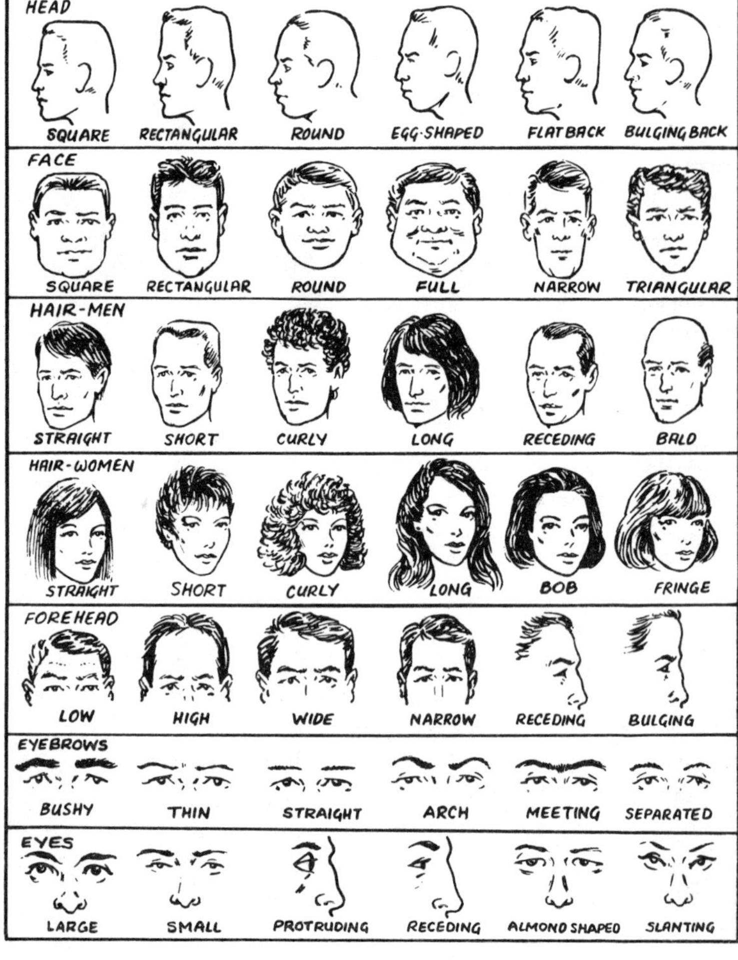

It is important to learn to concentrate on the permanent features of a person and not to pay too much attention to temporary ones. There is no point in remembering the colour of a woman's dress or the shape of her earrings, for example, because the next time we meet her she is almost certain to be wearing something else. Hair can also be a temporary feature – men can go bald, grow beards and moustaches or shave them off; women can change their hairstyle and colouring completely from one day to the next.

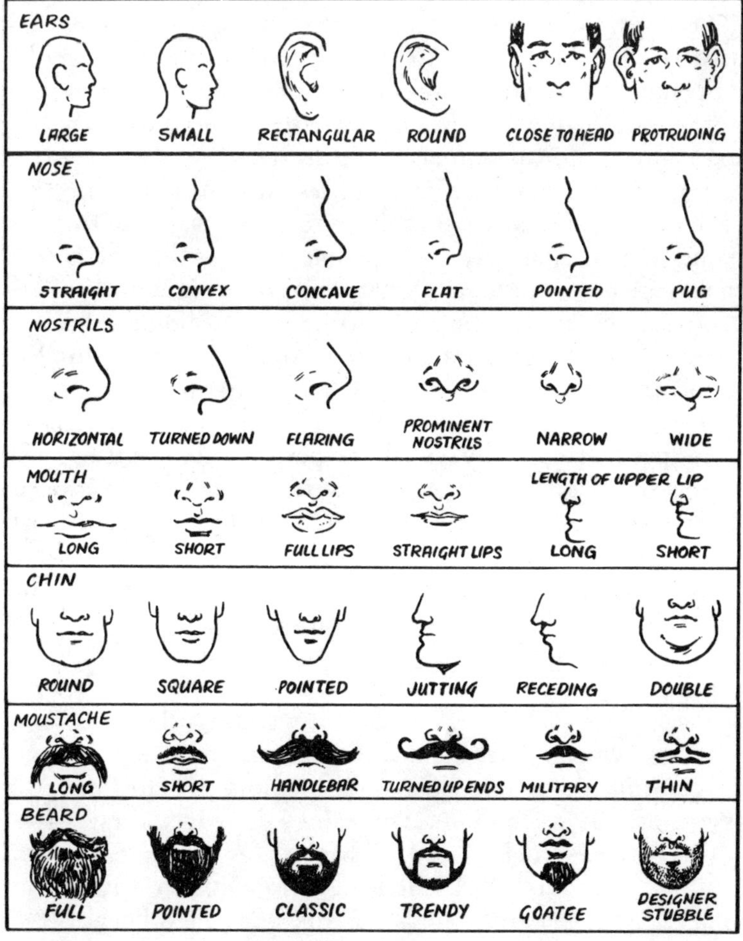

On the following pages there are photographs of twelve people, each with a name. They are real people, and have been carefully chosen in order to form a well-mixed group of men and women, young and old. Their names are not real, but were chosen at random. I hasten to add that the descriptions I have invented for them are wholly fictitious.

Together with the photographs you will find brief descriptions of each person's age group, character and general appearance together with some associations I have suggested for each name. They are of course only suggestions and you are free to make up your own.

Look carefully at each face, then read the descriptions and associations. Now turn to the page of illustrations in the Appendix where you will find the same twelve photographs, but without names and in a different order. See how many of the names you can remember correctly.

REPETITION. Once we have impressed somebody's appearance on our minds, we now have to do the same with their name. One reason why some people find this difficult is that they were never quite sure what it was to begin with, and we cannot hope to remember a name if we did not hear it correctly. The first step therefore is to make sure we do hear it correctly and if necessary know how to spell it.

If we did not quite catch the name when we were introduced, we can always ask the person to repeat it or spell it. People are quite accustomed to being asked 'Is that Thompson with a p, or Thomson?', for instance, or 'Is that Dennis with a double n?' People with unusual names are often willing to explain their origins, which helps fix the name in our minds. Even repeating a name silently to ourselves as soon as we have heard it is a useful way of making it easier to recall later on.

ASSOCIATION. Having made sure we know the name and what its owner's permanent features look like, we now have to commit these two items to memory by forming an association between them. This can be done in several ways.

If we meet somebody called Taylor, for example, we can immediately think of Elizabeth Taylor or Robert Taylor and imagine the person together with one or other of the well-known film stars. The more improbable such an association-image the better. If we meet a very respectable-looking person called Taylor we can have fun visualising him or her having a passionate close-up love scene with the appropriate star.

A Taylor can also be visualised as a tailor sitting cross-legged on a table sewing, just as a Smith can be imagined as a blacksmith bashing a piece of red-hot iron. This form of direct name-association gives us opportunities to make amusing and incongruous images, and these as we know are the images that we never forget.

There are four main ways of visualising names:

1 *Looking for Meanings.* I have already mentioned Taylor and Smith, and many other names are equally straightforward as far as visual associations are concerned. There are names which are also colours (Brown, Green, Black, White), and others that are also names of familiar objects (Hill, Field, Lane, Street) that automatically suggest associations. Then there are many names derived from professions or occupations such as Baker, Carter, Cook or Thatcher. In these cases, we visualise the person doing what their name suggests – baking some bread, pushing a cart, or whatever. There are even a few names that provide ready-made images involving some kind of action or feeling, such as Shakespeare, Makepeace or Lovejoy.

The origin of names is a fascinating study in itself, and the more we know about a person's name, especially if it is an unusual one, the easier it will be to remember it.

2 *Looking for Associations.* Many names have been immortalised by real or fictional people. We can never meet somebody called Holmes without immediately thinking of the great detective Sherlock Holmes, or a Churchill without bringing the familiar image of Sir Winston to mind. We can have fun pairing off the person we have just met with the famous namesake, imagining Mr Holmes playing chess with Sherlock, or Mrs Churchill partnering the former Prime Minister in a game of tennis.

Several names have equally strong associations from nursery rhymes, films or folklore. Examples include Simple

SID NUTTALL
Square head, determined mouth – tightly closed, deep lines from nose, small mole on right cheek, crinkly greyish hair.

Features: the lines at either side of the mouth are very strong and form part of the nostrils. The greyish hair is crinkly and wiry. (Age group: late 50s–early 60s.)

Association: he looks like he is chewing something: a **SEED**. The Seed turns into a **NUT**. He likes eating **ALL** kinds of nuts. You can also think of his head being a large NUT and his crinkly hair representing the fibres.

MARK HARRISON
Good-looking young man. Well formed straight nose, full lower lip, penetrating smallish eyes – well set apart.

Features: small black mole under left eyebrow, over nose and on right cheek. Slight bump on nose suggesting that it may have been broken at one time. These three marks form a diagonal line. (Age group: 25-30.)

Association: he has a small black mole or **MARK** near his eyebrow. The three MARKS were made by an animal whilst he was trying to talk to it. (He talks to the Animals!) Song made famous by actor Rex **HARRISON**. He could easily be the SON of Rex HarriSON.

MARJORIE BROWN
Square head, pudgy face, small straight lips, small light eyes – well set apart.

Features: distinct indentation in tip of nose and deep well over top lip. Small cheek lines either side of nose running towards mouth. A suggestion of a double chin. (Age group: mid–late 30s.)

Association: she looks overweight and is trying to slim. No more fatty butter – she eats **MARGE**. This is spread on a slice of brown bread; don't say HOVIS – say **BROWN!** She is eating a bacon sandwich and this makes us realise that with her round face, small eyes and stubby nose she looks like MISS PIGGY!

MAURICE JONES
Thick-set square head, leathery skin, very strong chin, large round-tipped nose with 'swept back' nostrils.

Features: thin lines on side of mouth, right ear lobe suggests a 'cauliflower' ear. (Age group: late 60s–early 70s.)

Association: he looks like a man who needs a drink. The look tells us that he is pleading with the unsympathetic barman for more ice (**MORICE**)! He was hoping for someone to join him for a drink – he looks unhappy because no one **JOINES** him.

ROB BUCHANAN
Rugged outdoor type, square chin with slight suggestion of cleft, broad nostrils, deep cheek lines, narrow 'weather-beaten' eyes.

Features: droopy eyelids and crinkly 'bags'. Small strong frown line between eyes. (Age group: mid–late 40s.)

Association: ARMED ROBBERY! He wanted to **ROB** a valuable **BOOK** not carrying a gun but a **CANNON**! He is screwing up his eyes (like prison bars) against the bright light – after spending years in a dark dungeon.

GEOFFREY BECKLEY
Oblong head, small round nose, smooth skin, stubborn mouth, eyebrows well set apart.

Features: penetrating dark eyes. (Age group: early 30s.)

Association: a highly successful **CHEF** (Jeff) donated his services **FREE** at a large open-air charity function which took place in a meadow. After cooking for hundreds of people he was exhausted and lay on his **BACK** in the meadow (**LEA**). His face appears smooth and white, as if covered in flour, and his dark eyes look like raisins.

Putting a name to the face

SID NUTTALL

MARK HARRISON

MARJORIE BROWN

MAURICE JONES

ROB BUCHANAN

GEOFFREY BECKLEY

JOAN JEFFARD

BRIAN KINGSLEY

EVE ROBERTS

GEORGE MAYBANK

RICHARD LANGFORD

MICHAEL ROBINSON

JOAN JEFFARD
Oblong head, straight well shaped nose, full determined mouth, eyes well set apart – large pupils.

Features: long narrow neck, natural outdoor look. (Age group: late 20s.)

Association: she has the looks of Joan of Arc. We can think of the highlight in her hair as a halo. **JOAN** of Arc was Saint **JOAN**. She is being burnt at the stake by a **CHEF** who is trying very **HARD** to set light to it! Her boyish look, determined expression and natural outdoor appearance make it easy for us to associate her with JOAN OF ARC.

BRIAN KINGSLEY
Square head, deep-set eyes, strong determined chin, four deep 'worry' lines, strong 'crow's-feet' at sides of eyes.

Features: small mole over left eye and on forehead. (Age group: mid 40s.)

Association: he looks very intelligent – with a good **BRAIN**. (BRAIN is an anagram of BRIAN.) The winner of numerous Competitions and Intelligence Tests, he is nicknamed 'the **KING**'. He is cunning and **SLY**. His wide brow has many lines, like a book. We can also imagine that they were caused by a heavy crown, worn on the head of a KING.

EVE ROBERTS
Oblong head, nose tilted upwards, wide nostrils, strong small line under nose, large, light, heavy lidded eyes.

Features: heavy folds under eyes and strong marks at side of mouth, on chin and on neck. (Age group: late 40s–early 50s.)

Association: when she was young – she wore **LEAVES** around her neck (like **EVE**) but now she wears ROWS OF BEADS which are tempting to **ROBBERS**. She has many wrinkles, especially around the eyes, which look like dried **LEAVES**, as the years have **ROBBED** her of her youthful looks.

GEORGE MAYBANK
Oblong head, narrow pointed chin. Long straight nose, large, clear, light eyes, suave and distinctive looking.

Features: freckles and distinctive grey hair. (Age group: early–mid 30s.)

Association: the freckles and spots on his face were caused by having to wear heavy make-up as a professional Male Model. He is known as GORGEOUS **GEORGE**. He has earned a lot of money and he can't make up his mind whether to BANK it or not. So he **MAY BANK** it (or he may not!).

RICHARD LANGFORD
Small square head, rugged look, well shaped nose, square chin, narrow smiling eyes.

Features: bushy eyebrows, joined over nose. (Age group: early–mid 20s.)

Association: he looks like an international young playboy who is **RICH** and works and plays **HARD**. He often travels abroad and speaks many **LANG**uages and drives a FORD – which he can well af**FORD**. His general appearance seems to confirm the above story line.

MICHAEL ROBINSON
Round head, balding, bushy eyebrows – knitted together, large teeth, heavy folds under eyes.

Features: many heavy 'crow's-feet' from sides of eyes. (Age group: mid–late 40s.)

Association: he looks like a jovial man and he is an amateur comedian who works every Friday in a club. He is used to speaking into a **MIKE** and has been offered the lead in the local pantomime '**ROBINSON** Crusoe'. His own jokes make him smile, which is obvious from the laugh lines around his eyes.

Simon, Larry the lamb, Jack and his beanstalk and the unfortunate Plain Jane. Saints and monarchs also provide convenient images, from St George and his dragon and St Joan leading the French into battle to King Alfred burning the cakes and William the Conqueror defeating the Saxons in 1066.

If there is no ready-made association as in the examples above, we can often make our own. Many names lend themselves to rhymes, and we can visualise Mabel sitting on a table or Ralph as King Ralph the Twelfth – we can be as ridiculous or unflattering as we like in our imagination.

3 *Changing Vowels or Consonants.* Names that have no obvious meaning in themselves and no immediate associations can often be made into something familiar by minor alterations to their spelling. Thus the name Kendall can be converted into Candle, which is something easy to visualise, Gannon can become Cannon, Dwyer can be turned into a Drier or Cohen into a Cone.

Look for a sound that is close to that of the name, and never mind how ridiculous the association is. Indeed, the more ridiculous the better. Think of somebody called Isaacs as clambering up a mountain with an Ice-Axe, or an Austin as a pair of Oars and a Tin, or a Noonan as a New Nun.

4 *Dividing Names into Units.* This is particularly useful with difficult names such as long or foreign-sounding ones that have no meaning at all in English. It will not always be possible to repeat the exact sound, but as long as it is near enough to the original to remind us of it, it will do. A name like Zielinski may seem difficult to remember, but it becomes much easier if we divide it to make Sealink-Ski. We can then visualise the person water-skiing across the Channel being towed by a Sealink ferry. Likewise we can imagine someone called Bhattacharya as Battering a Chariot.

People with unusual or difficult names are especially flattered when somebody remembers them correctly, and there is no need for them to know what kind of image we associated with them in order to help us do this, so we can let our imaginations run riot.

Very often names will divide themselves easily. We can

visualise someone called Penrose writing with a Pen made out of silver Rose, or a Burnett Burning a Net, a Saunders Sawing Doors or a Hollis making a Hole in Ice.

To summarise: we remember names and faces by using the I–R–A method, I for Impression, R for Repetition and A for Association. The basic rules are these:

1 Hear the name correctly, asking how to spell it if there is any doubt.
2 Get into the habit of repeating the name as often as possible soon after hearing it for the first time, either in conversation or silently to yourself.
3 Impress the essential features of the person's face on your mind. The chart on pages 92 and 93 shows you how to identify individual variations.
4 Form a pictorial association with the name either by looking for a meaning or an obvious association, or by dividing it into units.
5 Link the physical characteristics to the image that you have associated with the name. The more vivid or absurd the association the better.
6 Test yourself as soon as possible after meeting somebody for the first time by repeating their name. Write it down when you can, as this will strengthen the memory-link.

It is important to be able to put the face to the name as well as the name to the face. To practise this, write down all twelve names on a piece of paper, in any order. Go through the list without looking at the photographs and try to remember what each person looked like.

Remembering a face in a photograph is of course easier than remembering a live person. It is useful to practise with photographs, but you should move on as soon as possible to real people. The best person to start with is either the last one whose name you had difficulty in remembering, or the next person you meet after reading this.

An important aspect of associations of this kind is that once we have managed to remember a name and its face by the methods I have described, we will gradually be able to remember the name without needing to think of the absurd associations and images we invented. These are only necessary while we are fixing a name or face in the mind. Once they are fixed, we often no longer need the associations, so we can discard them.

13

FACTS AND FIGURES

What is the area of England? On what date was Abraham Lincoln assassinated? How high is Mount Everest, and where exactly is it? What is the world population and its annual increase? These are facts and figures that many people may have no need to know, and therefore no interest in learning. They are also examples of the kind of information which almost everybody must need to know at some point in a lifetime. In this chapter, therefore, I will explain at some length how I would set about memorising the above facts and figures, together with a selection of others. I must make it clear that they are merely given as examples. If they are of no particular interest, there is no need to learn them, although it is useful to know how to learn them if necessary. It is good to use these examples for practice.

Before attempting to memorise anything, we must be motivated. We must be able to answer the questions 'Is this fact or statistic important?' or 'What is my reason for wanting to remember this?' If we cannot provide satisfactory answers, we are not motivated and we will not remember. On the other hand, if we have to give a talk in which various facts and figures will be useful, if we are studying for an examination or an interview in which they will be essential, or if we merely have a natural thirst for knowledge and take pride in adding to it, then the motivation is there and recollection will follow. The first step in any memorising process, therefore, is to be aware of the reasons for wanting to remember something.

The next step is to decide which is the best method to use. In the case of individual facts or statistics, there are three choices. The first is to look at the item and see if there are any letters or numbers in it that have direct personal associations. To those born on 25 October, the numbers 25 and 2510 (or, in the United States, 1025) will always have special meaning, and be visualised simply as 'my birthday'. If we see a car number that contains our initials or the number of our telephone exchange, we feel an immediate association with that particular car. The effectiveness of such personal associations is proved by the number of people who can reel off names of famous men and women who were born on the same day as they were.

Many people are surprised to discover how many numbers and groups of letters have personal associations if they look for them. When no such immediate association comes to mind, we can look for one by seeing if the letters or numbers to be remembered can be matched with those of something we already know. For example, the number 47 may not have any immediate significance, but after a moment's thought we may find we know somebody who lives at 47, is 47 years old, or was born in '47. Again, it is surprising how many numbers and letters can be made personal with very little effort.

When neither of the above methods will do, we have to make use of such memory aids as acronyms or the Figure Alphabet to create imaginary associations, much as we do when making use of the Peg or Chain systems. It may be helpful for complete beginners if I describe at some length how I set about committing some facts and figures to memory. It must be emphasised that describing visual and mental associations on paper takes much longer than it does to form them in the mind, and it often sounds rather ridiculous. Nevertheless, it is precisely such 'ridiculous' images that have proved the most durable, so it seems sensible to make use of them.

I THE ASSASSINATION OF ABRAHAM LINCOLN

I will begin with the date of an historical event: 14 April 1865, the day on which President Lincoln was shot. First, I write down the date in figures: 1441865. Then I translate this into the Figure Alphabet, which gives me TRRTFJL. I divide this string of letters into groups, trying them out in various combinations of one, two or three until I find some words to fit them. As always, I choose the first that come to mind, provided they form a clear image. In this case, I come up with 14 (TR), 41 (RT) 8 (F) and 65 (JL) and take the words TEAR, RED, FOE and SHELL. (Remember that 1 can be T or D and 6 can be J or SH.)

It is now fairly easy to form a good visual link between seeing Lincoln being shot, shedding a tear, seeing red blood after the shooting by his foe and the empty shell of the bullet lying nearby. Thus the key-words tear, red, foe and shell are turned into a chain. To memorise it, I begin by adding the words A. Link at the start, to remind me that the date refers to Abraham Lincoln.

In some parts of the world such as the U.S.A. dates are written with the month first: 4/14/1865, so here is an alternative chain: the figures 4141865 are translated into RDRTFJL, which bring to mind the words RAIDER, TOUGH and JAIL and the image of a raider who is tough shooting the president and going to jail.

Here are our two memory aids for this particular event:

14/4/1865
A.Lincoln = A.Link
14 = TeaR
41 = ReD
8 = Foe
65 = SHeLL

4/14/1865
A.Lincoln = A.Link
414 = RaiDeR
18 = TouGH
65 = JaiL

2 THE AREA OF ENGLAND

The area of England is 50,362 square miles. To represent England, I visualise the national flag, the Union Jack. The numbers are translated into LZMJN which provides the words

LAZY and MACHINE. I then form a visual image of a lazy machine with a Union Jack fluttering above it. To remind myself that I am dealing with square miles I put the whole picture into a large square.

If I want to recall the area of England in square kilometres, which is 130,438, I make a different image based on the letters DMZ (130) and RMV (438). These give me the words DAMES and REMOVE and the image of a group of dames removing their clothes. To remind myself that they are dames and not just women or girls, I make use of the song 'There is nothing like a dame' from *South Pacific* and visualise my dames removing their clothes, which are red, white and blue, on a South Sea island beach. 'Clothes' brings the word 'kilos' to mind and establishes this statistic as being in square kilometres rather than square miles.

Area of England	=	50,362 square miles
England	=	Union Jack
50	=	LaZy
362	=	MaCHiNe
Square miles	=	image enclosed in a square

Area of England	=	130,438 square kilometres
England	=	Union Jack
130	=	DaMeS
438	=	ReMoVe
Square km.	=	kilos – clothes

3 MIXED NUMBERS

Many numbers that we have to remember consist of both letters and digits, such as car licence numbers in many countries. My friend Brian Barnes, who has worked with me on my memory seminars for many years, drives a car with the licence number C774 SNH. I dealt with this task as follows:

The letter C reminded me of CAR, the number 774 became KKR in the Figure Alphabet and immediately brought the word COOKER to mind, while for SNH I visualised a newspaper headline Splashes New Hat. Thus I formed a mental picture of Brian arriving in his new car to deliver a new cooker for my wife, and while demonstrating it splashing her new hat.

Brian's Car	=	C 774 SNH
C	=	Car
774	=	CooKeR
SNH	=	Splashes New Hat

To take another example from my recent experience, a student asked me to help him memorise his National Insurance number which was ZR 138364 B. He had never bothered to remember it himself, and a few days previously somebody had telephoned him to ask for it. He had wasted half a morning looking for it.

I divided it up, converted the numbers into letters and words, and in a very short time helped him to fix it in his memory for ever. The letters ZR reminded me of Zürich, and B reminded me of a Bank – something easy to associate with a Swiss city. The number 13 – 83 – 64 became TM – FM – SHR which suggested the words TIME, FAME and SHARE. Then I made up this story:

'You want to become a banker, and the best place to do this is Switzerland. You fly to Zürich to study for a long time until you achieve fame and can take a share in a major bank. There's your number – ZR (for Zürich), TIME – FAME – SHARE – B for Bank. To remind yourself that it is your National Insurance number and not any other kind of number, reinforce the story by seeing yourself taking out a large insurance policy before you fly, so that you will be insured while you are studying.'

Having made up this memory aid in a very short time, and without needing to write anything down, I proved how easy it is to memorise a fairly complicated number in a matter of minutes. Somebody suggested that I had been lucky in this case, so I immediately produced another way of remembering the same number to prove the point that all numbers are equally 'lucky' in this respect.

'ZR stands for Zoo Reptiles. 1 is To. 38 is MoVe. 364 is MaJoR and B is for Boa Constrictor. You are in the zoo reptile house and you have to move one of the main exhibits, a major boa. Once again, you need to be insured for such a dangerous task.

'Now you have a choice of two mnemonics for your National Insurance number. You will never forget it again.'

4 COMPOUND STATISTICS

Sometimes we need to remember certain facts and figures in association with other facts or figures. For example, we may want to know the height of Mount Everest (29,028 feet) and also where it is. This is not in India as a surprising number of people seem to think, but on the borders of Tibet and Nepal.

We can start by visualising the world's highest mountain going up and up for EVER to fix the name Everest in mind. The number of its height in feet translates into NBSNV which gives us the phrase NO BUS, NO VIEW. To include the two countries in our image, we can imagine ourselves having a Bet with a Pal and saying, 'I bet when you get there, you'll find there's no bus and no view', to which he replies, 'I'm going on foot' to remind you that the height is in feet.

Our mnemonic for the height and location of Mount Everest, then, looks like this:

TIBET NEPAL
(YOU BET A PAL)

Everest	=	Image of mountain rising up for EVER
Tibet/Nepal	=	tiBET your nePAL
2	=	No
90	=	BuS
2	=	No
8	=	View
Feet	=	Going on FOOT

For another example of a compound statistic, let us remember that the population of the world is 4,925 million and that it increases by about 80 million a year. Translating the first number we get RPNL, or RoPe – NaiL, and the figure 80 becomes FZ or FuSe. We need a visual symbol for world population, so we can imagine a POP bottle standing on one side of a globe, with a ROPE connecting the bottle to a large NAIL.

To include the annual increase, we can imagine a little FUSE tied to the bottle, going upwards in our mental picture to remind us that it represents an increase, and enclosed in a square to remind us that the figure is in millions. The whole picture is also surrounded by a square to remind us that the

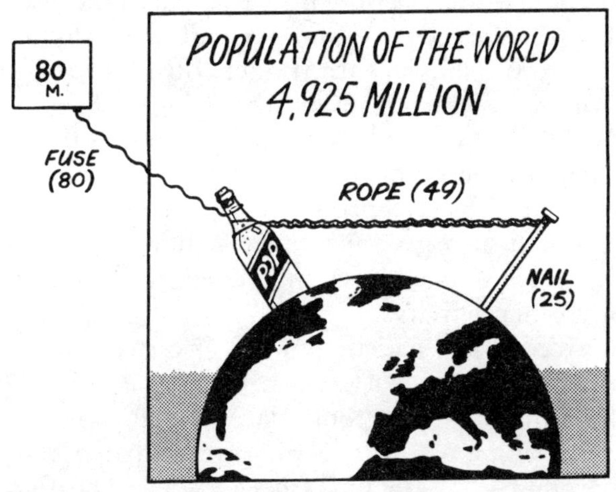

POPULATION OF THE WORLD INCREASES BY 80 MILLION PER YEAR

population figure is also in millions. For a figure representing the order of hundreds, I enclose the visual image in a triangular frame, for thousands, I use a circular frame, and for millions, a square frame. This simple code reinforces my image by reminding me what kind of number I am dealing with. In many cases it is not essential, since we will have a rough idea of the number anyway. We are not likely to think that the world's population is 49,250 or 49.25 million, because we should know that it must be a few billions.

Here is another example of a compound statistic: the value of goods imported into the United Kingdom in 1974 was £20.8 billion. To memorise this fact, in which there are fifteen digits involved, we can make abbreviations. If we use statistics on foreign trade frequently, we will know that the sum is always given in billions and we will know we are dealing with the year 1974 and not 1874. So we can reduce the number of digits to be learned to five: 74 – 208. Using the Figure Alphabet, this becomes KR – NZF, which gives us the words CAR – UNSAFE.

All we now have to do is visualise a car that is unsafe, which is all too easy. The brakes may have failed, or the steering wheel may have fallen off. When the time comes to produce the statistic, we only have to think of the year 1974 – or rather the year '74 – and we automatically find the association CAR. This in turn triggers off the word attached to it – UNSAFE, which translates back into 208.

One side-effect of producing a statistic out of the blue in a speech or a conversation is that we give the impression of knowing our subject thoroughly, perhaps better than we actually do. It also gives us added confidence in our own abilities, which is an essential ingredient in memory training as in any other activity.

With practice any statistic can be converted into an image very quickly. Here are a few examples:

1 The Battle of Crécy took place in 1346. We need only remember 346, as we have a rough idea that it was somewhere around the 13th or 14th centuries. The figure 346 becomes MARSH (M,R,J or SH) and we associate Crécy with CRESS. We then visualise large marsh covered with cress.

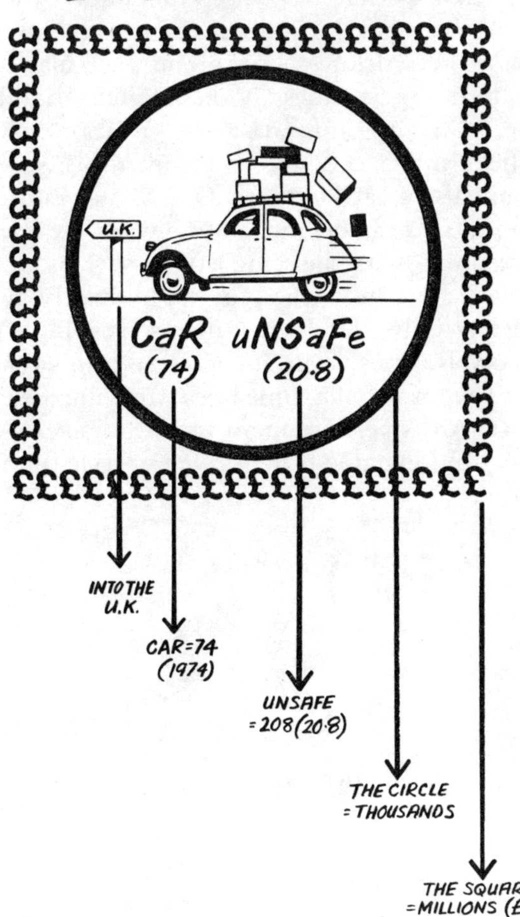

2 Bombay is 4,890 miles from London by air. The figure becomes RFPS, or ROUGH PASS. We link this to a BOMB to provide an effective image, if a rather alarming one.

3 Exact location of Peking (now Beijing) is 39.50N., 116.20E. These figures become MoB LooSe – DeTaCH NewS. The N. and E. conveniently come together in the word NEWS. As for Peking, we can associate it with a Chinaman peeking out of a window!

4 Area of Poland: 121,000 square miles. The figure 121 becomes TNT, or TENT, and nothing is easier to associate with a tent than a POLE. If we need to reinforce the image to remind ourselves that the figure is 121,000 and not 12,100 or 12.1 million, we enclose the image in a circular frame.

5 The five largest cities in the United Kingdom after London are Birmingham, Glasgow, Liverpool, Manchester and Sheffield, in that order. To remember this, we need only take the initials of each city – B,G,L,M,S – and make up a phrase to fit. This can be done in two ways: by a sentence of words beginning with the same letters, such as British Girls Like Marmalade Sandwiches, or more simply by making words using only the letters themselves plus the most suitable vowels. Thus we can turn BGLMS into BIG LIMES, and visualise a row of very big lime trees stretching from one city to the next. An American might prefer BIG LIMOS (short for limousines) and imagine being driven in style to each city in turn.

BiG LiMoS

14

The Basic Rules of Memory

For many people, the most frequent task given to the memory is that of recalling everything to be done on a certain day. There are those who are quite satisfied to write out lists of the day's actions and appointments on the back of an envelope, which serves well as a memory aid until the day when it is lost or left at home. An alternative would be to make use of the various techniques described in this book. They are no more time-consuming than writing things on bits of paper, they serve to keep the memory fit and active day by day, and above all they do not get lost.

Let us take a typical list of a day's appointments and things to be done:

1	Post a letter	6	Look up train times
2	See bank manager	7	Return library book
3	Visit dentist at 10.45	8	Collect coat from cleaner
4	Buy stationery	9	Telephone plumber
5	Book theatre seats	10	Repair window latch

The first thing to do is decide in which order these are to be done. As in the case of preparing a speech, this is a question of seeing what has to be done first and what should be left until later. The rest can then be arranged to involve the minimum of running around. Let us suppose that we cannot reach the plumber during the day, and we need to take our time repairing the window latch. These two items move naturally to the end of the list. The dentist's appointment must be near the beginning, and the bank is next door, so that can be done just before the visit to the dentist. The theatre seats and train times can be dealt with during the lunch hour. Better post the letter first thing after leaving home, and leave the coat until later to avoid having to carry it around all day. The list soon arranges itself in a convenient order. Each item should now be reduced to a single key-word, as follows:

1	Letter	6	Train
2	Bank	7	Book
3	Dentist	8	Coat
4	Envelope	9	Plumber
5	Theatre	10	Window

These can be linked by either the Chain or the Peg Systems, making up a story using all the words in their original sequence, or associating each one with the rhyming 1–gun, 2–shoe list. There may be a problem in using the Chain system for a task of this kind, since it works properly only when the sequence of items cannot be altered, as in a speech or a presentation where it is essential that the items are recalled in the right order. With a day's appointments, however, plans may have to be changed. The theatre box-office may be closed, or the bank manager might not be able to see us when we call. Thus the chain would fall apart, and at the end of the day it would be necessary to go through the whole original chain to find the missing link. Therefore the Peg system would be the right one here.

An interesting and important feature of this method is that if one of the items has to be left out for some reason, it will stand out in the mind like the proverbial sore thumb. I have noticed that when I am testing groups of people on lists of as many as thirty peg-items, everybody always knows exactly which numbers have not yet been called out. Therefore, by arranging a day's appointments as a peg rather than a chain, there is no difficulty in remembering something that has been left undone.

Very often, it is the trivial things that we forget. There is no point in remembering to call somebody as soon as we get to the office if we cannot remember who it was, or making an appointment with a busy bank manager and then forgetting one of the most important questions we wanted to ask him. Let us suppose in the first case that we had to call our accountant. All that need be done is to choose an image that represents him, such as a pound or dollar symbol, and combine this with an image of the office. We can visualise ourselves arriving at the office to find the telephone ringing twice as loudly as normal, to remind us that our call is an urgent one. Then we look at the receiver and see it in the shape of a £ or a $. This image will act as a reminder to call somebody connected with money.

If it is essential to post a letter early, a visual association can be formed beforehand between the act of leaving home and the pillar box. Imagine the letter as a kind of magic carpet, with yourself sitting on it and flying along the road right into the pillar box. Exercising the mind in this way creates a visual link between the object (letter) and what has to be done with it (posted), which is far more effective than merely repeating, 'I must remember to post the letter'. As for writing things on backs of envelopes, devotees of this traditional habit must admit that there are situations in which this cannot be done. It would hardly be good manners to produce a list in the middle of a smart dinner party in an attempt to steer the conversation in the desired direction!

Notes on bits of paper are also of no help in such common predicaments as forgetting where we have left something. Nothing is more infuriating than having to go out in a hurry and finding that the car keys are not where they should be. To avoid frustrations of this kind, which can have serious consequences, all that is required is to discipline ourselves to form automatic associations at a moment's notice. I keep my car keys together with most of my other keys on hooks which are labelled, and when I get home I automatically put them on their hook. If I come home one day to find the telephone ringing, I might go to the phone with the keys still in my hand and then put them down by the vase in the hall. The phone call might distract me by giving me some unexpected news or obliging me to go and do something urgently as soon as I have rung off. I then have to go out in a hurry – and where are those wretched car keys?

I instantly remember that they are beside the vase. How? Simply by having formed a visual association between keys and vase as I put them down. It only took a fraction of a second to visualise myself dropping the keys into the vase with such force that the vase shattered. Or I could have imagined the keys starting to grow into flowers. In this way, despite the distracting phone call, the keys were not lost. They might not have been in their proper place but the image-link was – in my memory store.

A useful and simple rule is to make some kind of visual association every time something is put down that will be required later, such as a hammer or a garden tool. These have a way of getting lost if we are distracted by the telephone or somebody at the front door, so these associations have to be made very quickly indeed. This is a discipline that must be acquired to avoid the tiresome business of trying to retrace our steps until we remember where we were the last time we were using that particular tool.

Although there are numerous rules for memory improvement, I have devised a list of ten basic ones:

1 Think in pictures. This is the most basic rule of all. Convert a word – any word – into an image, and do this instantly. Once something is seen in our imagination, it is remembered.
2 Link objects together. This can be done either as a sequence with the Chain or Stack systems, or as individual images linked to a peg method (rhyming, alphabet or place). Cut out all inessential details and stick to the single image.
3 Make the pictures concrete. Think of familiar objects, the more personal the better. It is easier to think of our front gate or our tape recorder than of an imaginary front gate or any old tape recorder. If there is a need to visualise something we do not possess, it is simply acquired in the imagination and made one's own.

4 See objects in action. A dynamic image is easier to remember than a static one. A leaking pen or a tourist riding a bicycle in a race are more easily remembered than an ordinary pen or a tourist standing still and holding a bicycle.

5 Make the pictures striking. The more startling, unusual and ridiculous they are, the better. Use the kind of imagery to be found in cartoon films, as when an animal is squashed flat by a steam-roller and later pops back to its normal shape. A normal everyday image such as a table with a glass on its top will not be remembered as easily, since there is nothing particularly memorable about it.

6 Increase or decrease the size of objects. Instead of an ordinary table and glass, make the table so huge that the tiny glass on top of it is out of reach. Or have a gigantic glass balanced on a miniature table. This kind of Alice in Wonderland imagery is what sticks in the mind. Distortion of any kind is a very effective visual memory aid.

7 Exaggerate the number of objects. Hundreds or thousands of bricks are easier to remember than one brick. This is another way of distorting an image.

8 Animate the image. By bringing people into a mental image, it will become easier to remember. It will be still easier if the people are personal friends or well-known celebrities.

9 Test the memory regularly. (This applies especially in the early stages of memory improvement.) A certain amount of revision and practice is necessary to prevent the mind and the memory system from stagnating. Regular practice, whenever a suitable occasion arises, also helps increase confidence by proving to ourselves that we can remember things when we want to.

10 Strengthen the image. This can be done in many ways as already described. Having spent much of my professional career in film and television studios, I like to make use of camera techniques to help rein-

force my images, seeing them as big close-ups, wide-angle or travelling shots, zooming in and out, and so on.

The effectiveness of these basic rules may be tested in everyday experience. Let us suppose that you were unexpectedly asked to describe some of the cars you saw in the street yesterday. You may have seen hundreds, yet I doubt if you could describe a single one accurately unless it happened to be a very special one, such as a well-preserved vintage model. Now imagine sitting on top of a bus next to a person who suddenly exclaims, 'Oh, there's been a terrible accident. Don't look!' What is the first thing you do? You look, of course! It may only be for a second, catching a glimpse of the wreckage, the victims and many other details, but one second is long enough to impress that gruesome image on the mind for ever. Several years later, if somebody were to mention having seen a nasty accident that day, the reaction might be, 'You should have seen the one I saw in . . .' whenever it was, perhaps ten or twenty years ago. You then describe it in detail.

Comic or absurd images are just as easy to recall. In the 1950s, a group of Cambridge undergraduates managed to haul a small car up to the roof of the Senate House in the middle of the night. It stayed there for several days and became a tourist attraction. I doubt if anybody who saw that comic, surrealist image of a Baby Austin parked neatly on the roof of a large building in the main street will ever forget it. The same car might have been parked in front of the same building for weeks without anybody giving it a thought. Putting it on the roof instead was enough to make it memorable.

To help remember the ten basic rules above, I have devised a simple chain of images which I call The Fairground Story. It also serves as a fine example of how to make up a chain, each word in capitals being an image made from a key-word in each rule, linked with as much action as possible:

You are going to a fairground, and as you approach it the first thing you notice is a lot of PICTURES for sale, hanging on a chain-LINK fence. Their weight is pulling the fence away from the CONCRETE posts, so workmen are getting ready to do some repairs. Their foreman shouts, 'Let's have some ACTION'. The men begin STRIKING the posts with sledge hammers. Their job is made difficult because of the SIZE of the fairground and the large NUMBER of PEOPLE getting in the way as they queue for the TEST your STRENGTH sideshow.

15
A Question of Memory

The effectiveness of the memory-improvement methods described in this book has been proved over and over again, not only by me and the numerous people who have attended my seminars, but by countless individuals who have tried them for themselves over the past two thousand years. Yet there are still those who allege that memory aids amount to a form of cheating, and that the methods used are ludicrous and embarrassing. If it is considered cheating to obey a law of nature, then I can only express gratitude that such a convenient and practical form of 'cheating' exists. Everybody uses it, whether individuals are aware of doing so or not. Everybody without exception uses some kind of personal memory aid, whether it is a housewife going shopping, a student preparing for an examination or a businessman making a list of appointments. Writing things down on backs of envelopes or learning them parrot-fashion are memory aids of a kind, but no such elementary method can be as effective as the systematic techniques that have been tried and tested for centuries and are still being refined and modified.

Memory, as we have seen, is largely based on association, and this will take place spontaneously if it is outstanding in some way. It may be aroused by a beautiful view, a song, a poem or a play, or by a dramatic event such as a road accident. Whatever the circumstances, anything that has made sufficient impact on our minds will always stay with us whether it is pleasant or unpleasant. It is the memories formed in this way that are the easiest to recall.

Other memories are recalled in more subtle ways. How is it that we are able to look at a certain view and state confidently that we have never seen it before, or meet somebody we know we have never met before? This can only be done if we have remembered every view we have ever seen and every person we have ever met. This does not mean that we can instantly recall every one of those views and people, even if we have impressions of them stored in some distant corner of our memory banks. In most cases, such impressions will have been stored without strong associations and therefore will be difficult to retrieve consciously.

Many of the impressions and items of information we absorb through each of our senses all the time will never be needed again. Others will be needed, and therefore we have to make sure that they will be retrievable instantly on demand. When there is no spontaneous strong association, we have to provide one. Experience has shown that the only practical way to create artificial and strong associations is to exaggerate them and make them as ludicrous as possible. If this seems trivial to some and beneath their dignity, so be it. I have yet to hear of a workable alternative method.

I have often had to face scepticism and bewilderment at the start of one of my memory seminars. It can certainly be embarrassing for senior executives to be asked to play childish games and see themselves or their colleagues in absurd situations in order to remember things. However, it is soon found to be quite enjoyable, and, more importantly, it is also found to work. There is never any scepticism remaining at the end of the first session of a seminar.

People tend to be suspicious of simplicity. When I am asked to a meeting to explain what memory improvement is about, there are always those who are looking for highly sophisticated and complicated methods. Sometimes they are surprised when I tell them that the methods I use are all based on very simple ideas. Ironically, it would make things easier for me if they were more complicated than they are. Their very simplicity is a handicap, though I always prove my point by demonstrating how quickly and easily they can be made to work. Memory aids are not a form of cheating, but a way of helping our memory systems to perform more efficiently by encouraging them to make better use of techniques that come naturally to them. They will only seem trivial to those who are unaware of these natural and instinctive techniques.

There are many popular misconceptions about memory. One is that it fades with age. This can happen, but in most cases it has been allowed to fade by letting the motivation lapse. Anybody who has an interest in life stays young in mind if not in body, and the memory also remains young. I have known amateur magicians in their eighties who are as motivated and alert as any youngster, keeping up their interest in their hobby until their very last days, and surprising everybody by appearing so youthful. I have had delegates of eighty and even ninety at my seminars, and they have been able to manage all the exercises as well as anybody else.

Older people can have very clear memories of events that took place many years ago when their motivation was strong. Such memories have been constantly reinforced by repeated recollection, photograph albums and souvenirs, and remain as vivid as ever. The same people may not be able to remember what they had for lunch that day because they were not motivated to remember. It did not mean very much to them. It is the motivation that fades with age, not the memory. The problem is compounded by the fact that we tend to programme ourselves to believe that memory deteriorates with old age. Once this is believed, it will come true.

Another widespread misconception concerning memory training is that it is only useful to stage performers or those who wish to entertain at parties. This is a more serious misconception, and it is totally false. One businessman I know came to a seminar of mine because he had been recommended by his own secretary. He kept noticing that when he was talking to clients on the telephone while she was in the room, she would constantly correct him or remind him of something he should have mentioned. It turned out that she had attended one of my previous seminars and found that her overall mental performance had improved in all kinds of ways as a result. She had become a good listener as well as a good memoriser, and was able to take in everything she heard, check it with the information in her memory store, and spot any discrepancy at once.

The surprising truth is that people who have gone through a memory-improvement programme invariably improve all round, just as this secretary did (as eventually did her boss). Once people become programmed to realise that they have the ability to visualise numbers, or to make associations with names and pictures, they then do this automatically. As they get better and better at it, they gain confidence, and as the results of their self-training create a more favourable impression so they become even more motivated. It is all a question of programming, motivation and confidence, and one inevitably leads to the others.

Many of my employers have been large multinational companies who can well afford any course or instructor on any imaginable subject. The fact that I have been employed again and again by the same companies, in some cases over periods of fifteen to twenty years, indicates that the methods I teach produce the desired results. Just as physical exercise leads to improved stamina, muscle power and general fitness, mental exercise tends to make people perform better at any task that requires thought, whether this is speaking in public, organising a complex operation, or making plans of any kind. Once we earn ourselves a reputation for either physical or mental performance, we are naturally motivated to perform even better.

If we find ourselves on the wrong escalator in the Underground, it can be quite difficult to turn round and go back. We are carried up or down by a momentum beyond our control, and it requires determined effort to overcome it. In any self-improvement programme, the essential first step is to make sure we get on the right escalator – that is positive motivation. Having taken this step, the rest becomes much easier than might have been imagined.

It is all too easy to become motivated in the downward direction, either by being told that something cannot be done or merely by assuming this. Fortunately, it is just as easy to direct the motivation upwards, as readers of this book will know. (Nobody who was downwardly motivated would have read it.) After trying the exercises and practising the techniques that have been described, it will be found that from now on your motivation can only be in the upward direction.

EXERCISES

1 Chain and Stack Systems (Ch.7). Practise linking short lists of items using either the Chain or the Stack System. Visualise the lists both forwards and backwards.

2 The Peg System (Ch.9). Learn the rhyming pegs from 1–Gun to 10–Hen until you are quite familiar with them. Test yourself until each number immediately brings the right word and image to mind.

Make up some personal place-pegs based on your house, office, or a familiar walk.

Make up your personal peg alphabet, using familiar objects and as many with personal significance as possible.

3 The Figure Alphabet (Ch.11). Learn the Figure Alphabet until each digit immediately brings its corresponding consonant-sound to mind. Practise it with numbers that are important to remember, such as a bank card. Make sure that every new word-image is thoroughly learned before moving on to another. Keep a special area of your memory for items that need remembering on a long-term basis.

4 Look up a telephone number you have to call frequently and convert it by any of the methods described in this book into a phrase or series of images.

5 Facts and Figures (Ch.13). Take any fact or figure that you need to remember and turn it into an image or sequence of the kind described here. Think of the last item you could not remember when you needed to, and start with that one.

APPENDIX

THE PEG SYSTEM

THE PLACE METHOD

Use places familiar to you, e.g.:

Rooms in your home, an individual room, your place of work, public buildings, streets, a map of the world:

HOME	ROOM (e.g. Kitchen)	OFFICE
Front Door	Door	Desk
Hall	Table	Chair
Living Room	Sink	Telephone
Dining Room	Cooker	Typewriter
Kitchen	Refrigerator	Filing Cabinet
Broom Cupboard	Pedal Bin	Photocopier
Cloakroom	Radiator	Waste Bin
Landing	Washing Machine	Window sill
Bedroom	Cabinet	Plant
Bathroom	Window	Light Fitting
Loft		

THE RHYMING METHOD

1	Gun	5	Hive	8	Gate
2	Shoe	6	Sticks	9	Wine
3	Tree	7	Heaven	10	Hen
4	Door				

THE ALPHABET METHOD

A	Apple	J	Jug	S	Snake
B	Book	K	Keg	T	Table
C	Cat	L	Lake	U	Umbrella
D	Dish	M	Mat	V	Vine
E	Egg	N	Net	W	Watch
F	Flag	O	Oak	X	Xylophone
G	Goal	P	Pipe	Y	Yacht
H	Hat	Q	Queen	Z	Zoo
I	Ink	R	Rose		

For each letter of the alphabet, choose a word beginning with that letter which, *for you*, suggests a good, distinct picture. (The words listed are only examples.)

REMEMBERING NUMBERS

EXAMPLES 0 – 150: KEYWORDS

0	sea sew say zoo hose ace see ice easy ooze wise sow saw
1	tea tie hat wood head hood toe tow wit hit toy dough
2	wine Noah inn hen win gnaw neigh wane
3	mow ham hem hymn home hum may yam aim
4	row ray rye ear air hare wire year hire hear wear worry
5	law ale eel whale wheel lie low hole hull heel heal hail
6	shoe ash chew jaw wish hedge show jay age hatch
7	key cow egg ache oak hag hack wick wig guy week
8	view ivy foe wife heave wave heavy weave hive
9	pie pea hoop whip pay bee buy boy bow bough web
10	toes dice dose doze deuce toss
11	toad date deed tot tight diet tit dot
12	tin ton dine town tone tune din dean
13	time team tomb tome dome dummy dumb dim atom
14	tree tyre tear heater water door deer draw
15	dial doll towel tool dole till tail
16	teach touch Dutch dash dodge ditch
17	tug tag dig dog dock duck teak tick deck

18 dive toffee dove tough deaf dive
19 top tube tap dip type tip
20 news nose nice once niece Nessie ounce wince
21 nut gnat knot need net hand wand hunt ant knead
22 nun nanny neon noon anon
23 name gnome numb
24 narrow Nero winner near
25 nail kneel Nile nil
26 notch nudge hinge inch gnash niche
27 neck knock ink nag
28 knife navy knave nave
29 nib nip nap knob
30 mouse maze moss miss maize mass amaze
31 mat mud mad mood meat moat maid
32 man moon money woman yeoman mine moan omen
33 mummy maim mime memo
34 marrow moor hammer marry mire
35 mail mule mill meal mole mile
36 match mash mesh
37 mug mike mac
38 move muff movie
39 mop mob imp hemp
40 rose rice erase race rise horse
41 rat road rod root write heart
42 rain run warn yarn arena
43 rum room ram rhyme arm
44 roar rower rear
45 reel rail roll royal
46 rich rash arch rajah ridge
47 rock rag rack rake rook
48 roof rough rave raffia
49 rope robe rob rub ruby
50 lace lass louse lasso
51 loot lute light lid lead lady
52 lion lane line lean loan
53 lamb loom lime limb
54 lorry lyre lair lure

55 lily lolly loyal
56 lodge ledge lash leash latch
57 log lock lake lick leg
58 loaf life leaf laugh
59 lip leap
60 cheese chess juice chase choose
61 jet jade shade shed cheat judo
62 chain shine gin join shin chin
63 gem jemmy chime jam
64 jar cheer shear share chair
65 jewel jail jelly shell chill
66 judge gee-gee hashish
67 jug cheque chick joke shack
68 shave chef chief jive sheaf
69 ship chip shop chop jab
70 case gas axe cosy goose quiz
71 cat cut gate goat kite cod
72 can cane gun cone queen
73 comb cameo game gum
74 car gear core cry grow
75 coal goal kill gill quill
76 cage cash catch gash cosh
77 cake cook cog keg
78 coffee cafe cough cave
79 cap cab cub cube
80 face vice fuse vase
81 fight foot vat vote fat food
82 fan phone fun vane fin van vine
83 foam fume fame
84 fire free fair fry
85 file foal fly vail
86 fish fetch fudge voyage
87 fig fag fake fog vague
88 fife viva
89 fob fib fop
90 bus bass pass baize
91 bed bat pat bet pad

92 bone bin bean pin pan pony
93 bomb beam poem puma
94 bar bear beer pear pour
95 ball bell bill pill play pail pole
96 bush badge page push patch
97 bag pack pig peg book
98 beef puff pave buff
99 baby pipe pub bib
100 disease

EXAMPLES 00 – 09

00 sauce seize oasis
01 seat stew soda side city sweet
02 sun son sign swan
03 sum swim seam
04 sore sour seer czar
05 seal sail sell cell swallow
06 sash siege switch sage
07 sock sack sago sick
08 safe sieve sofa save
09 soap soup spy sweep

KEY WORDS FOR NAMES

FORENAMES

Alan	Al ale	Angela	angel
Barry	berry	Ann	ant
David	Goliath	Barbara	barber
Eric	hayrick	Elizabeth	queen
George	gorge	Florence	floor ants
Harold	Harry hairy	Jane	chain
Ian	iron	Katherine	wheel
James	jam	Margaret	mark crate
John	join	Maureen	mooring
Michael	microphone	Philippa	flipper
Norman	gnaw man	Sheila	shield
Philip	Phil file	Winifred	wine fried

SURNAMES

Austin	oars tin
Bhattacharya	batter a chariot bat a chair
Briggs	bricks
Cassidy	gassy tea
Churchill	Winston
Cohen	cone
Crowhurst	crow hearse crow hoist
Doyle	doll doily
Ellis	eel ice
Gilbert	gull bite kill bird
Hickey	high key
Hoyle	oil
Isaacs	ice axe
Jennings	gin inks chaining
Jones	joins
Keating	key tin
Kendall	candle
Mackay	mac eye
Noonan	new nun
Oakley	oak leaf
O'Rourke	oar rock
Quinn	queen
Rutherford	rudder ford
Saunders	sawing doors
Thorpe	thaw
Vaughan	fawn van
Watts	light bulb
Westcott	waistcoat
Williams	wheel jams
Zachary	sack carry saccharin
Zielinski	ceiling ski Sealink ski

Putting a name
to the face